SARGON THE MAGNIFICENT

BY

Mrs. SYDNEY BRISTOWE

Author of " THE OLDEST LETTERS IN THE WORLD."

LONDON :
THE COVENANT PUBLISHING CO. LTD.
6 BUCKINGHAM GATE, S.W.1
1927

CAST OF DOUBLE-HEADED BUST
in the collection of Prince Orsini, Rome. Supposed date about 20 B.C. (City of Nottingham Museum and Art Gallery.)

[See p. 110.
[Frontispiece.

CONTENTS

PART TWO

INTRODUCTION

About thirty years ago in a series of lectures a certain German professor, himself a higher critic, announced his belief in the Divine inspiration of the first chapters of Genesis; his regret at the attacks being made upon their authenticity by other professors; and his conviction that if a certain discovery could be made it would largely help to counteract those attacks. He apparently did not expect that such a discovery would be made; but I hope to show that when the cuneiform inscriptions found in Babylonia and now available for anyone's inspection are studied from a new point of view, that discovery is ours.

In support of this new point of view, extracts from works by leading Assyriologists are quoted in the following pages, and their translations of the inscriptions are given. It can scarcely be thought presumptuous on my part if I suggest a new application of those inscriptions considering that the deductions already drawn from them are indeterminate and unconvincing. While taking advantage of them I make bold to suggest that their decipherers, like others before them, may sometimes have " failed to see the wood for the trees."

That the writers, from whose works I quote, hold different views from my own naturally makes any of their evidence that supports my views the more convincing because it is involuntary. Since the history which they have deduced from Babylonian inscriptions is admittedly conjectural, and rests upon a certain hypothesis described by one of them as almost incredible, it is well that some other hypothesis should be tested, and I claim that my new version of Babylonian history rests upon a much more reasonable one.

That a new interpretation should be welcome is suggested by Professor Sayce's words:

" Both in Egypt and Babylonia, therefore, we are thrown back upon the monumental texts which the excavator has recovered from the soil, and the decipherer has pieced together with infinite labour and patience. . . . The conclusions we form must to a large extent be theoretical and provisional, liable to be revised and modified with the acquisition of fresh material or a more skilful combination of what is already known." (*The Religions of Ancient Egypt and Babylonia*, p. 3.)

And also by Professor T. Eric Peet, who writes:

" Archæology can in no sense be termed an exact science, that is to say, its conclusions rarely follow with mathematical certainty from its premises, and indeed but too frequently they do not rise above the level of mere nebulous possibilities or probabilities. This state of things is partly to be accounted for by the very nature of its subject matter, but also, in the opinion of the writer, by the fact that archæologists have hitherto made no attempt to come to any kind of agreement as to the conditions which must be satisfied by a train of archæological reasoning in order that it may acquire cogency. We are doubtless all to blame in this, and in our defence it can only be urged that the constant accumulation of fresh material has tended to distract our attention from a really critical use of the evidence already available." (*Journal of Egyptian Archælogy*, 1922, No. 8.)

Neither fresh material nor a skilful combination is offered in this little work, but a new combination of the facts already known about ancient Babylonia taken in conjunction with the Bible Records which I claim to be the Master-key to the problem of the ancient civilisation of that country.

I have been asked to say that the Council of the B.I.W.F. does not associate itself with my views about the preadamites and the Deluge.

LIST OF ILLUSTRATIONS.

SARGON THE MAGNIFICENT

I

" Great floods have flown
From simple sources, and great seas have dried
When miracles have by the greatest been denied."

IT has been said that nothing worth proving can be proved,
and certainly this applies to the theory put forward in this
little book ; but I hope to interest the reader in my attempt
to show that the stories told in the first chapters of Genesis
harmonise with the researches of modern archæologists, and
provide a key to some otherwise unsolved problems.

It has not been easy to marshal the mass of evidence collected
here, and a certain amount of reiteration of arguments and
facts has been unavoidable ; but I dare to think that after a
careful and open-minded consideration of these pages some at
least of my readers will be convinced that that mysterious
personage, the great Babylonian monarch Sargon of Akkad,
was none other than the first murderer in history—Cain. By
showing that Cain and Sargon were one and the same and thus
linking up the sacred and profane histories of the ancient world,
I hope to refute the modern teaching that the Bible story of the
Garden of Eden is mythical.

Up to the present the Babylonian inscriptions and drawings
have interested comparatively few people, but those who
accept my theory that Sargon of Akkad—who plays so large a
part in them—was Cain, will agree that they should be of
universal interest ; for, granting this, there emerges from the
tangled mass of evidence provided by those inscriptions and
drawings a vast and sinister figure whose influence upon mankind far eclipses that of any other character in secular history.
I shall endeavour to show that to his superhuman knowledge

must be attributed the pre-historic civilisations now known to have existed in different parts of the globe, as well as the savage barbarism which accompanied them ; and that to him must also be attributed the institution of idolatry—that poisoned chalice " the Golden Cup " of Babylon, which " made all the earth drunken " in olden times and whose dregs have still power to work mischief among men.

Although modern scholars seem to ignore the possibility that Cain may have influenced the history of the ancient world, three notable writers at the beginning of the Christian era (St. Jude, Josephus and Philo) suggested that Cain's influence was evil and enduring ; while a modern poet reminds us that, somewhere in the world, Cain's descendants must have worked out their tragic destiny.

Lord Byron makes Lucifer say to Cain :

> " First-born of the first man
> Thy present state of sin—and thou art evil—
> Of sorrow—and thou sufferest—are both Eden
> In all its innocence compared to what
> Thou shortly mays't be ; and that state again
> In its redoubled wretchedness, a Paradise
> To what thy sons' sons' sons, accumulating
> In generations like to dust (which they
> In fact but add to), shall endure and do.—
> Now let us back to earth ! "

And back to earth we too must come. To make poetry about Cain is one thing—to install him suddenly in secular history, or to try to do so, is another. This book is inevitably contro- versial and my task has been no light one in writing it, for I try as it were to build upon a site already occupied and to clear the site while building. When I add that the building to be cleared away is, in plain language, certain views set forth by well-known writers, my difficulties will, I am sure, be fully appreciated. The courage required for such a formidable under- taking comes from my conviction that while the views I oppose are entirely based upon modern discoveries, my theory derives support not only from those discoveries, but also from the Book of Genesis. This conviction, which I regard as my strength, will undoubtedly be looked upon by some people as a weakness; for it is now the fashion to decry the first chapters of Genesis, to ignore the possibility of their Divine Inspiration, to treat their historical information as fabulous, and to consider it unintelligent to believe in anything of a miraculous nature.

It is taught, sometimes even by the clergy, that the Old Testament stories owe their origin to the pagan traditions of Babylonia, but my object is to show that the beliefs and institutions of ancient Babylonia, and of other lands as well, confirm the historical truth of the Bible instead of discrediting it. I maintain that unless we accept its stories as true history we are, although " ever learning . . . never able to come to a knowledge of the truth."

The men who ignore these stories are, however, accepted as authorities, they carry weight and have the public ear; it may indeed seem bold to question their conclusions. These, however, fortunately for my purpose, do not always agree and are often indefinite and liable to be changed at any time to suit new theories brought forward. Sir James Frazer, for instance, has lately thrown doubt upon the prevailing opinion held by Assyriologists that the Babylonian myths upon which the Genesis stories are supposed to be modelled were evolved by the first inhabitants of that land, and has suggested instead that they may have originated in Africa, travelled thence into Babylonia and later on have found their way into the Hebrew literature.[1] This conjecture he bases on the recent discovery that traditions reminiscent of that literature, such as those of a fall of man and a serpent tempter, exist among the tribes of the Tanganyika Territory in Africa. Considering, however, that the earliest rulers in Egyptian history are now believed to have gone into Africa from Asia[2] it is surely, on the face of it, much more probable that those stories were taken by them into Africa, and there corrupted into the grotesque traditions found among the African tribes.

By comparing and contrasting the Biblical and Babylonian

---

[1] Gifford Lecture, Edinburgh. November 21st, 1924.
[2] *Ancient Egyptians*, p. 150. Dr. Elliot Smith. *The Religions of Ancient Egypt and Babylonia*, p. 22. Professor Sayce, etc.

stories, and by bringing forward fresh evidence (or at least evidence which has so far passed unnoticed), I hope to show that the Bible stories *do not* owe their origin to Babylonian myths and legends, but that they are, on the contrary, true history.

II

THE BABYLONIAN INSCRIPTIONS

BEFORE looking for Cain in the Babylonian inscriptions a short account of those inscriptions, of their arrival in England and America, and of the effect they produced there, must be given.

On the site of the palace of King Assur-bani-pal, where once had stood the city of Sennacherib King of Assyria, thousands of brick tablets have been found, upon some of which, inscribed in cuneiform characters, are mythological versions of the stories told in the Book of Genesis about the Creation of the World, the Garden of Eden and the Deluge. The date of the tablets is thought to be about 700 B.C. and they are believed to be copies of much older writings which Assur-bani-pal had caused to be collected from all parts of his kingdom and stored in his library. Many of these fragments were brought to England towards the end of the last century, and the late Mr. George Smith of the British Museum was the first to transliterate and make known to the public these " Genesis stories."

Although these Babylonian stories are replete with the names of gods and goddesses, they are in some ways so like those in the first chapters of Genesis that they were joyfully received at first as new evidence of the truth of the Bible records. Professor Kittel of Leipzig writes :

> " When, therefore, George Smith was fortunate enough to discover in the year 1887 cuneiform inscriptions containing the account of the Flood, the expressions of delight beyond the Channel and Atlantic knew no bounds. Sermons from the pulpit and whole columns from the Daily Press were filled with accounts of the discovery . . . every doubt of the

sceptic and every sneer of the mocker, it was thought, in regard to the Bible would be utterly and inevitably confounded."

In 1903 he wrote :

" A very different picture presents itself before our eyes to-day.   A period of sobriety and in many cases of depression has followed that of jubilation and enthusiasm.   In the family of oriental studies Assyriology is the latest born.   It need not be a matter of wonder, therefore, if in individual instances representatives of the new knowledge should not have always been able to shake off the child-like love of sensation.   Formerly men were attracted to the study of the monuments with the hope of finding arguments on behalf of the Bible : now, the contemporaries of Nietzsche and Haeckel find there is a much greater prospect of attention being directed to the new learning if it should succeed in adducing evidence against both the Bible and Christianity." (*Babylonian and Oriental Excavations*, pp. 12-13.)

This is surely a grave accusation, although so dispassionate, in tone.   Professor Kittel was one of the first and keenest German higher critics : his work, *The History of the Hebrews*, was even considered too destructive by our own higher critic Professor Kelly Cheyne.   The fact that Professor Kittel retained his faith in the Divine revelation of the Old Testament stories after analysing and comparing the Biblical and Babylonian versions, should carry weight with the most sceptical. An examination of the Babylonian story of the Creation of the World shows the justice of his opinion that the Assyriologists, who first suggested that the writer of Genesis borrowed his ideas from Babylonia, did not really believe that proposition, but only wished to advertise their new branch of science. Professor Kittel's summary of the Babylonian story is as follows :

" When on high the heavens were not named, and below the firmament was not yet designated . . . then were the gods formed. . . . In the beginning the chaotic waters, called Tiamat, held sway. They were the enemies of order. As the gods wished to create from these an orderly world, Tiamat arose as a dragon against them. Ignominious terror seized the gods, until Marduk the god of the Spring-sun, undertook to battle with the monster and its companions. He conquered it, cut the dragon into two halves, and made out of one the heavens, out of the other in like manner the earth, upon which he then brought forth animals and men." (*Babylonian and Oriental Excavations*, p. 39.)

The effusion, of which this summary gives some idea, is equalled in absurdity by what is called the Sumerian story of the Creation of the World, also found in Babylonia, and considered to be the origin of the above version and that given in the Old Testament.

To appreciate the absurdity of the " Sumerian version " of the Creation, etc., Professor Leonard King's work, *Legends of Babylon and Egypt*, should be studied. The first lines are typical of all " Sumerian " writings :

" When Anu, Enlil, Enki and Ninkharsagga
  Created the blackheaded (i.e. mankind), to produce
  The animals, the four-legged creatures of the field,
  They artfully called into existence."
  (*Legends of Babylonia and Assyria*, p. 56, L. King.)

That the sublime account of the Creation given in Genesis was inspired by such utter nonsense is surely unthinkable. The perfect agreement of the Bible account with the discoveries of modern science should, one would think, convince anyone that the writer was divinely inspired. Since that perfect agreement is not always realised the subject is dealt with in Appendix A.

In answer to Professor Delitzsch's insinuation that the Biblical account of the Creation is only a re-arrangement of Babylonian myths, and that some Israelitish scribe's conception of God was inspired by the Babylonian deities, Professor Kittel writes :

B

" It must, moreover, be always borne in mind that it is psychologically inconceivable that the lower forms of religion, which are glibly assumed to be the original—such as fetishism, totemism, animism, etc.—could have come into existence without the previous conception of a higher power behind them, that is, of God Himself. That a stick, or a stone, or an animal could be regarded as God cannot have been a primary, but only at most a secondary conception. It is certain that to primitive man a stone in the first instance was a stone, wood was wood, and animal animal, and he could with his own eyes see that these things had no inherent power of themselves to make alive, or kill, or produce growth. But when once he had obtained the conception ' God,' he might readily suffer it in course of time to degenerate, so that this power, while it is invisible, became associated in his mind with visible things, such as trees, stones, or animals. . . . In the words of the late F. Max Muller—words often quoted and frequently with contempt, but never yet refuted— ' The human mind would never have conceived the notion of gods if it had not first of all conceived the notion of God '." (P. 52.)

Professor Kittel's final conclusion is that the Bible and the Babylonian stories all come from the same source and have a common origin from which, proceeding in two streams and subjected to independent development, they issue respectively in a nature myth and a monotheistic religion with an ethical base. He describes as follows one way in which the attacks upon the Divine origin of the Bible might be successfully combated.

" There is one problem whose solution would well reward the cuneiform investigator, would surpass all previous discoveries and excuse all disillusions and false conclusions, and that would be the discovery that in the grey dawn of history there were actually men in existence who still possessed . . . the inheritance of an exalted knowledge of God, which had at some time or other been imparted to mankind. For that stones, or trees, or even dead men should have awakened in mankind the earliest presentiment of God, or should have attracted it to themselves, we cannot allow ourselves to be persuaded, no matter how frequently and how loudly this theory is maintained." (*Excavations in Babylonia, etc.*, p. 60.)

Professor Kittel has hit upon the only way, as it seems to me, of refuting the attacks upon the authenticity of the Genesis stories. He saw clearly that what was wanted to support the Bible testimony in these incredulous days was involuntary evidence from ancient pagan monuments. Although he appears to have had little hope of that evidence being found, I claim that it has been discovered inadvertently and passed over almost without comment, because its full significance has not been recognised. The fact that men who possessed the knowledge of God existed in Babylonia in the " grey dawn of history " is proved by a few cuneiform tablets, whose existence I conclude was unknown to Professor Kittel. Their inscriptions strongly resemble the Hebrew literature and betray the knowledge of One God, although they were found among hundreds of other tablets of an entirely polytheistic character.

These few monotheistic inscriptions (which will be given later) are said by Assyriologists to be copies of much earlier ones, dating back to before 2000 B.C., and it is remarkable that the pagan priests who inscribed them finally (and in some cases left their mark upon them) in the seventh century B.C. allowed them to come down as evidence that the knowledge of God had once existed in their land, where at that time hundreds of false gods were worshipped. When Professor Kittel says " This is an investigation which cannot be pursued to a definite conclusion by historical means " I cannot agree with him ; my object is to show that, on the contrary, historical means are at hand if a fresh interpretation is given to the Babylonian inscriptions ; and the first question to be discussed is how did the knowledge of God arrive in Babylonia, and who took it there. We gather from the Bible that the exalted knowledge of God was handed down by the descendants of Seth, the third son of Adam and the ancestor of Noah ; and it seems probable that after the Deluge it was preserved by Noah's descendants in Northern Syria, and made known to Moses by his father-in-law Jethro the Midianite who, it seems, may have come from that part of the world.[1]

On the other hand, there is ample evidence in the Babylonian inscriptions, if my new interpretation of them is accepted, to prove that the other stream of knowledge was taken into Babylonia by none other than Cain, that it there became obscured by the system of fables and myths now known as mythology, and that it was Cain who originated that system by establishing the first false gods.   If this new interpretation is accepted we have substantial evidence that one of the earliest Biblical characters played a prominent part in the secular history of the ancient world, and we can reject the assertions that the first chapters of Genesis were derived from Babylonian myths.   Like the pieces of a picture puzzle the evidence lies before us—waiting to be put together.   Excavators and decipherers have provided the pieces of the puzzle, but it is for us to make the picture.

---

[1] *The Hittites*, p. 9.   Dr. Cowley suggests the possibility that the Midianites of the Bible were the Mitanni of Northern Syria mentioned in the Amarna Tablets.   Higher Critics admit the probability that Jethro greatly influenced Moses.   We read : The legislation on Mount Sinai (Horeb) which apparently occupies a very important place in tradition . . . is really secondary . . . more prominence is evidently to be ascribed to the influence of the half-Arabian Jethro or Hobab " (*Ency. Brit.*, Ed. XI, " Moses.")   Jethro the Midianite is also called Hobab the Kenite, and we read : " Variant tradition would seem to show that the Kenites were only a branch of the Midianites." (*Ency. Brit.*, Ed. XI., Kenites.)

III

Two of the most recent writers upon the Babylonian inscriptions unintentionally support Professor Kittel's opinion that the Genesis stories came down in "two streams," and also my theory that one stream came down through the descendants of Seth and the other through Cain in Babylonia. Before quoting their remarks, however, I must explain why they call the first possessors of the "very ancient knowledge" Semites; for if they were the family of Adam they should, of course, be called after him and not after Shem (or Sem), who lived much later.

The Cambridge History tells us that the problem of the term Semitic is acute, that it is

> "More convenient than accurate and is derived from Shem, a son of Noah the hero of the Deluge."
> (Vol. I, p. 184.)

but it offers no solution of the problem. Surely it is the use made of the word which is puzzling, and not the word itself, for nothing could be more self-evident than its meaning "related to Shem or his reputed descendants."[1] Why, for instance, do Assyriologists describe Sargon of Akkad as Semitic, when, according to monumental evidence, he lived about 3800 B.C.; long before Shem's time? The ambiguous use of the word Semite can be traced to two German professors[2] who, about the year 1790, proposed that thenceforth the word should mean oriental. Unfortunately, later scholars, following the German lead, use the word Semitic at one time (especially in connection with languages) as meaning oriental and at other times as meaning related in some way to Shem, and this

[1] *Imperial Dictionary.*
[2] *Century Dictionary.* Semitic.

causes confusion. If, as I claim, Sargon was Cain, he should be called an Adamite rather than a Semite, and his subjects who are called Sumerians or Akkadians by Assyriologists[1] on account of the geographical terms Sumer and Akkad found in the inscriptions were, of course, pre-Adamites.

Poets and painters have depicted Cain as going into exile accompanied by an Adamite wife and family, but the Bible leads us to infer that before the birth of Seth only Cain and Abel had been born to Adam and Eve. We are prepared, therefore, to find that Cain had settled among a non-adamite race when he built a city and founded a family; and, as we shall see, modern discoveries go to prove this.

[1] Professor Waddell says that the word Sumer was used in Babylonia " solely as a territorial, and never apparently as an ethnic title," and quotes Professor Sayce's opinion that it was the same word as Shinar (the Biblical name for Babylonia). *Asiatic Review*, April, 1926.

IV

PRE-ADAMITES

HERE another digression becomes necessary. It is generally thought that the Bible teaches that Adam was the first human being, but in that case it would seriously contradict itself in the fourth chapter of Genesis, although that chapter contains (as one of the latest dissectors of the Bible shows)[1] one unbroken narrative. In that chapter Cain says :

> "My punishment is more than I can bear. . . . Behold, thou hast driven me out this day from the face of the earth . . . and it shall come to pass, that every one that findeth me shall slay me." (Authorised Version.)

Since, according to the Bible, Cain and his parents were the only Adamites in existence at that time, he must be understood to refer to pre-Adamites—unknown people among whom he was being driven forth ; and we are told that a mark was put upon him as a protection against those people. This shows that, although we may assume that Adam was the first man into whom God breathed a " living soul," he was not the first human being upon the earth.

As Cain is afterwards said to have built a city and called it after his eldest son, he must presumably have gained an ascendancy over those pre-Adamites, although he went alone amongst them. If, as Professor Sayce thinks probable, Babylonia was the country to which Cain journeyed[2] and if, as the same authority suggests, the first inhabitants of that country were blacks,[3] it is easy to imagine Cain, a white man

[1] Dr. Moffatt.
[2] See p. 27.
[3] " As, however, M. Dieulafoy's excavations on the site of Susa have brought to light enamelled bricks of the Elamite period on which a black race of mankind is portrayed, it may mean that the primitive population of Chaldea was blackskinned." (*Hibbert Lectures*, p. 185. 1887.)

endowed with superhuman knowledge and physique and rendered invulnerable by some divine talisman, taking command over those pre-Adamites; and that he did so seems proved by the fact that he built a city and called it after his son Enoch.

We see, therefore, that the Bible sanctions the belief in pre-Adamites, and that the oldest monuments in the world indicate that they were blacks. In fact both the Bible and modern science confirm these assumptions. The Bible, by showing that only eight of Adam's race were saved in the ark, demands a belief in a previous black race to account for the existence of blacks in later history, for how could the Ethiopian who, the prophet remarks, could no more change his skin than the leopard his spots, have descended from Noah? Science, by discovering the fundamental physical differences between the black and white races, has shown the fallacy of the old idea that they had a common origin,[1] and that either the white race was evolved from the blacks or the blacks were sunburned brothers of the white men.

My claim that the black race was a separate creation previous to Adam may be thought to contradict St. Paul's statement that God " hath made of one blood all nations of men "; I must, therefore, explain my belief that the Apostle only referred to white people—my contention being that the word man (used synonymously with Adam in Genesis II)[2] distinguished Adam from the pre-Adamites, and has continued to distinguish his descendants from the black race all through history. Do we of the present day ever call a negro a man without using the adjective black? In 2 Sam. xix, 12, Isa. xlvi, 8, and Cor. xvi, 13, the word man is used as a distinction; just as we say, "like a man," "be a man," or, "he is a man."

The fact that the word " Man " meant a thinker,[3] suggests

[1] " In the texture of bone, the architecture of the skull, the nature of the asymmetry of the body and the character of the variations—in these and many other respects there is evidence of the profound gap that separates the Negro from the rest of mankind." (*Ancient Egyptians.* Elliot Smith. p. 73.)

[2] " Adam, in Hebrew as in Assyrian, signifies ' man '." Sayce. *The First Book of Moses called Genesis.* Appendix.

[2] *Century Dictionary.* Man.

[3] Professor Max Muller writes : " Man, a derivative root, means to think. From this we have the Sanskrit Manu, originally the thinker, then man.' (*Lectures.* Vol. I., p. 425.)

that the " living soul " breathed into Adam raised him above some previously created race. In Sanscrit literature the first man is called Manu or Menu.[1] It will be shown later that the monuments support my theory that the word " man " distinguished Adam's race from the pre-Adamites.[2]

Just as the discovery that a black race existed at the beginning of history[3] supports the Bible's testimony that although Adam was the first man he was not the first human being—so does the continued existence of that black race prove that the Deluge was not universal. Noah's sons were surely white men, therefore the " Hamites " of later days must have been the result of the intermarriage of Ham's family with some black race which had survived the Deluge.

In the Bible story of the Deluge the meaning of the writer has obviously been misinterpreted by the translators of the authorised version. The Hebrew word *eretz* has been translated by them " the earth " or " all the earth," which has caused us to think that the Bible teaches that the Deluge was universal, and destroyed every human being and animal in the whole world with the exception of Noah's family. The word *eretz*, however, also means " country," " land " or " district," and is used in that sense in the story of Cain, who says :

> " Behold thou hast driven me out this day from
> the face of the earth."

In this sentence the word *eretz* is translated by Ferrar Fenton " this land," and by Dr. Moffat " the country," which are obviously better translations.

One commentator says of the word *eretz* :

> " As in many of these passages it might seem as
> if the habitable globe were intended, the use of so
> ambiguous a term as ' the earth ' should have been

---

[1] " Menu-Swayambhuva is certainly Adam ; and he is described as preceding by several generations Menu-Satyvrata, who is as certainly Noah." (*Origin of Pagan Mythology*. Vol. II, p. 102. Faber.)
" Mens. Under this name the Romans personified intelligence and prudence." (*Dictionary of Classical Antiquities*. Nettleship.)
[2] p. 156, p. 136
[3] See p. 15 and *Ancient Egyptians*. G. Elliot Smith.

avoided and the original rendered by ' land,' as in Lev. xxv, 23=Isaiah xxiii, and elsewhere." (Kitto's *Cyclopædia of Bible Literature*. Earth.)

That the writer of Genesis did not intend to teach that the Deluge was universal can scarcely be doubted, for if it had been universal and if only Noah's family had been preserved out of the whole world, not only would the existence of the black races have been inexplicable but also that of the descendants of the pre-Noachian giants (the Nephilim or monsters) found in Palestine in the time of Moses and Joshua.[1] We may therefore conclude that when Noah was told that " all men " and " all flesh " upon the " earth " were to be destroyed only the Adamites and the animals in the district inhabited by them were referred to. Wild beasts would naturally have been exterminated in that district, so we may dispense with the curious picture of every kind of wild beast processing into the ark, for obviously Noah was only commanded to preserve the animals useful to mankind, which had been allowed to remain in the district populated by the Adamites.[3] It is surely easier to accept these explanations of the seeming contradictions in the Book of Genesis than to allow that the Bible contradicts itself.

It is hoped that this digression will serve its purpose in persuading the reader that both the Bible and Science, as well as common sense, justifies the hypothesis that Cain settled among black pre-Adamites in " the Land of Nod " (Babylonia) after his expulsion from the land of his birth.

[1] Num. xiii, 33.   Joshua xii, 4, and xiii, 12.
[2] See Appendix.
[3] See Appendix B.

UNINTENTIONAL SUPPORT FOR MY THEORY

THE latest writers upon the Babylonian inscriptions unintentionally support my theory that while the knowledge possessed by Adam was preserved in Seth's branch of the family, in the form made familiar to us by the Bible, it was taken into Babylonia by Cain and there parodied. To appreciate their support, however, we must substitute the word Adamites for the word Semites in the following quotations, for the writers are speaking of people who lived before Shem and who therefore cannot accurately be called Semites.

Dr. Clay, in 1923, published a book in America, in which he says :

> " Assyriologists, as far as I know, have generally dismissed as an impossibility the idea that there was a common Semitic tradition, which developed in Israel in one way and in Babylonia in another. They have unreservedly declared that the Biblical stories have been borrowed from Babylonia, in which land they were indigenous. To me it has always seemed perfectly reasonable that both stories had a common origin among the Semites, some of whom entered Babylonia, while others carried their traditions into Palestine." (*The Origin of Biblical Traditions.* A. T. Clay. P. 150. 1923.)

Professor Delaporte of Paris, who holds the same opinion, published the following statement in 1925 :

> " If the theory that the first Semites to settle among the Sumerians were a branch sprung from the group of the Western Semites be confirmed . . . then the Pan-Babylonian thesis falls to the ground completely. The civilisation of Israel would then no

longer be wholly a reflection of that of Babylon ; the traditions preserved in the Book of Genesis would not be importations from Chaldea ; on the contrary, it would be the Semites who introduced them in the last stage of their eastward wandering to the Sumerians and the latter who adopted them.'' (*Mesopotamia,* p. 355.)

It will scarcely be denied that these views pave the way for my claims that Cain took the knowledge (which he shared with his parents) into Babylonia, and that the inscriptions which have been regarded as the origin of the Genesis stories are the result. They also support Professor Kittel's opinion that the knowledge imparted to man in the beginning has come down in two streams, on one hand through the Hebrews, and on the other through the Babylonians.

VI

SARGON OF AKKAD

My claim that Cain was the great Sargon about whom Babylonian inscriptions have much to say, invites adverse criticism and perhaps ridicule from those who see no connection between early Babylonian history and the first chapters of Genesis. Since, however, George Smith (the first decipherer of the cuneiform inscriptions) and Professor Sayce[1] identified the Babylonian hero Izdubar or Gilgames with the Biblical Nimrod, and since Noah appears under another name in the Babylonian story of the Deluge, it can hardly be regarded as incredible that Cain should also appear in the inscriptions, especially as the name Sargon may, as we shall see, be the Babylonian for " King Cain."

Professor King considered that the Babylonian and Egyptian legends were based upon true history ; he writes :

> " There is another element in many of their legends which must not be lost sight of, and that is the substratum of historical fact which underlies the story and was the nucleus around which it gathered. Echoes from the history of the remote past may perhaps be traced . . ." (*Books on Egypt and Chaldea*, Vol. 4, p. 198.)

To invite at the outset a certain amount of confidence in my theory I mention here the following indications which will be

[1] In the *Hibbert Lectures*, 1887 (p. 8), Professor Sayce says : " There are grounds for thinking that Mr. George Smith was right in seeing in him [Gilgames] the prototype of the Biblical Nimrod." He seems, however, to have changed his opinion, for in *Religions of Ancient Egypt and Babylonia* (p. 447) he says that Assyriologists were " long seduced " into trying to identify Gilgames with Nimrod, but that " it was not with him but with the Greek Herakles that the Babylonian hero was related." My suggestion is that both these pagan heroes may have represented Nimrod, for, as I show later, the Biblical characters appear under different names in the mythologies of Babylonia and Greece.

dealt with more fully later. To begin with, Professor Sayce's opinion that Cain may have built the Babylonian city of Unuk or Erech shows that there is nothing improbable in my claim that Babylonia was the Biblical " Land of Nod " to which Cain journeyed ; and allowing that Cain built that Babylonian city, the fact that Sargon is said in inscriptions to have reigned in it, at once connects the two.[1]

According to another authority, the civilisation of Babylonia arrived there suddenly and unaccountably, as Cain would have done ; while the Babylonians relate how Sargon arrived mysteriously in Babylonia ; that he was a gardener when young and reigned in later years over people called " the men of the black headed race "[2]; all of which agrees with the assumption that he was Cain (the tiller of the ground) who settled among black pre-Adamites.

Another important fact is that Sargon's language (Ancient Babylonian) resembled Hebrew, which was presumably that of Cain. Professor Sayce writes :

> " There is, however, one Semitic language which has the closest affinities to Hebrew and this is also the language in which we possess records older than those of the Hebrew scriptures. I need hardly say I am referring to Assyrian [i.e. Babylonian]."[3] (*Hibbert Lectures*, p. 46.)

Amazing things about Sargon have been gathered from the Babylonian inscriptions, and at least one portrait of him has been found, which is thus described :

> " Only one sculptured monument of Sargon has been recovered, it is a large triangular monolith found at Susa ; the king, according to Semitic fashion, has a long beard reaching to his waist, heavy moustaches and his long hair is rolled into

[1] *Cambridge History.* Vol. I, p. 404.
[2] *Hibbert Lectures*, 1887, p. 27. (Or *The Black-heads.*) See p. 28.
[3] " It is usually called the Assyrian, after the name of the country where the first and most important excavations were made ; but the term ' Babylonian ' would be more correct, as Babylon was the birthplace of this language and of the civilisation to which it belonged." (*Ency. Brit*. Ed. XI. Semitic Languages.)

NARAM-SIN

Stele found in Babylon.

[See p. 23.

SUMERIAN ROYALTIES

[See p. 39.

The above illustrations are reproduced from King's " A History of Sumer and Akkad," by permission of the Publishers, Messrs. Chatto and Windus.

[Face p. 23.

a huge chignon at the back of his neck." (*Cambridge History*, Vol. I, p. 408.)

Professor King says that if

"Any one point in early Babylonian history was to be regarded as certainly established it was the historical character of Sargon of Agade. . . . Sargon's reign forms the most important epoch in the early history of his country." (*Sumer and Akkad*, p. 216.)

Dr. Hall writes:

"Few monarchs of the ancient world are so well known to us moderns who are interested in these subjects as Sargon of Agade, and we may say that to the Babylonians he was their hero of heroes, their Menes, Charlemagne or Alfred the Great." (*Ancient History of the Near East*, pp. 20-30.)

In the Cambridge History we read:

"The fame of Sargon was such that a range of mountains in the Lebanon region from which frankincense (lupanu) was obtained, was named the Mountain of Sargon. . . . Sargon divided his vast empire from the lower sea to the upper sea, from the rising to the setting of the sun into districts of five double hours march each, over which he placed the 'sons of his palace.' By these delegates of his authority he ruled the hosts of the lands altogether." (Vol. I, p. 406.)

My suggestion is that these "sons of his palace" were Cain's own descendants, and that they helped him to rule the inferior race (the pre-Adamites). The inscriptions show that Sargon made war against people of his own race[1] and took prisoners with whom he populated some of his cities. It is probable that he had Adamite wives and that some of those " sons of his palace" were pure Adamites,[2] as the monuments show his son Naram Sin to have been. (See illustration.)

We read that Sargon

"Made successful expeditions and that with the

[1] *Sumer and Akkad*, p. 249. L. King.
[2] See Appendix C.

conquered peoples of those countries he peopled Akkad." (*Stories of the Nations: Chaldea,* p. 205. Ragozin.)

Professor King writes:

" In some versions of his new records Sargon states that ' 5,400 men daily eat bread before him ' . . . though the figure may be intended to convey an idea of the size of Sargon's court, we may perhaps see in it a not inaccurate statement of the total strength of his armed forces." (*Legends of Babylon and Egypt,* p. 9.)

The following statements show the highly civilised state of Babylonia in the time of Sargon of Akkad.

The Times History says:

" Babylonian art, however, had already a high degree of excellence ; two seal cylinders of the time of Sargon are among the most beautiful specimens of the gem-cutters' art ever discovered. The empire was bound together by roads, along which there was a regular postal service, and clay seals which took the place of stamps are now in the Louvre bearing the names of Sargon and his son. A cadastral survey seems to have also been instituted. . . . It is probable that the first collection of astronomical observations and terrestrial omens was made for a library established by Sargon." (Vol. 1, p. 362.)

We also find that " transparent glass seems to have been first introduced in the reign of Sargon." (*Ency. Brit.* Vol. 3. Ed. 2. Babylonia.) And Professor King writes:

" The Babylonians divided the day into twelve double hours ; and the Greeks took over their ancient system of time-division along with their knowledge of astronomy and passed it on to us." (*Egypt, Babylon and Palestine,* p. 18.)

Professor Sayce tells us that :

" Centuries before Abraham was born (about 2000 B.C.) Babylonia was full of schools and libraries, of teachers and pupils, and poets and prose writers, and of the literary works which they had composed." (*Monumental Facts, etc.*)

Sargon's voyages by sea and conquests on land will be described later in the words of Assyriologists, who feel forced to accept as history what the inscriptions say about them, although to those who do not identify Sargon with Cain they naturally seem almost incredible. *The Cambridge History* says :

"It seems impossible to explain away the voyage of Sargon across some part of the Mediterranean, and naturally Cyprus was his first objective." (Vol. I, p. 405.)

One writer quotes an inscription in which Sargon says :

"For forty-five years [the number of years is admittedly undecipherable] the kingdom I have ruled, and the black heads (or black) race I have governed. In multitudes of bronze chariots I rode over rugged lands. I governed the upper countries (Assyria, etc.). Three times to the sea I have advanced." (Ragozin's *Chaldea*, pp. 205-207.)

The same writer remarks :

"He is also stated to have made successful expeditions to Syria and Elam, and that with the conquered peoples of those countries he peopled Akkad, and built there a magnificent palace and temple, and that on one occasion he was absent three years when he advanced to the Mediterranean, and . . . left there memorials of his deeds, returning home with immense spoils." (*The Worship of the Dead.* Colonel Garnier. P. 398.)

It is evident that no ordinary human being, not even a Charlemagne or an Alfred the Great, could have evolved, during his lifetime, this great civilisation ; and so Assyriologists find themselves bound to attribute its evolution to the inferior race among whom (according to the inscriptions) Sargon arrived suddenly and over whom he eventually reigned. **My**

C

own contention is that nothing short of Cain's arrival in Babylonia, his longevity (Jewish tradition says he lived more than 700 years), and his super-human knowledge can account for the magnitude of the achievements ascribed to Sargon, and the advanced civilisation and culture of Babylonia.

VII

SARGON—KING CAIN

THE strongest evidence of the identity of Sargon with Cain comes from the Babylonian inscriptions and will be given later, but solid grounds for holding it are supplied by several authorities who had no idea of suggesting that identification ; a fact which makes their testimony all the more valuable.

To begin with, the city which, as we read in the fourth chapter of Genesis, was built by Cain in the " Land of Nod," and which he " called after the name of his son Enoch," was probably, according to Professor Sayce, the Babylonian city Unuk or Erech excavated by him.

> " If I am right in identifying Unuk with the Enoch of Genesis, the city built by Kain in commemoration of his son." (*Hibbert Lectures*, 1887, p. 185.)

And

> " Erech appears to have been one of the centres of Semitic influence in Babylonia from a very early period." (*Hibbert Lectures*, 1887, p. 185.)

The Cambridge History says of Sargon :

> " His career began with the conquest of Erech." (Vol. I, p. 404.)

Reasons for thinking that it began with the building, rather than the conquest, of Erech are given later. The facts that Erech is called " the old city " and the " place of the settlement " (see p. 72), and that, according to Professor Sayce, the name of " Unuk is found on the oldest bricks "[1] help to identify Erech (or Unuk) with the Enoch built by Cain.

[1] *Hibbert Lectures*. Index.

As to the sudden and almost miraculous arrival of civilisation and culture in Babylonia, Professor King writes :

" We have found, in short, abundant remains of a bronze culture, but no traces of preceding ages of development such as meet us on early Egyptian sites." (*Egypt, Babylon and Palestine,* p. 28.)

This, of course, harmonises with my belief that Cain, protected by some divine talisman, arrived suddenly in Babylonia, bringing with him the supernatural knowledge acquired by his parents.   One writer, expressing his astonishment at the high grade of civilisation and culture which is known to have existed in Babylonia in the time of Sargon, writes :

" Surely such a people as this could not have sprung into existence as a Deus ex Machina ; it must have had its history—a history which presupposes a development of several centuries more." (*Times History,* Vol. 1, p. 356.)

The expression " Deus ex machina " paraphrased by Dr. Brewer into " an intervention of a god or some unlikely event," is curiously appropriate in connection with my belief that the Babylonian civilisation was due to the sudden advent of Cain with his marvellous knowledge.

The first Adamites were presumably superhuman in both mind and body, which would account for the great ages to which they lived.   We can easily imagine, therefore, how quickly Cain (divinely protected by some mysterious mark) would become the leader, teacher and absolute lord and master of an inferior race.   As if in support of this suggestion Professor Sayce writes :

" Slavery was part of the foundation upon which Babylonian society rested." (*Babylonia and Assyria,* p. 67.)

The bronze age of Babylonia, which arrived so suddenly and, from a modern scientific point of view, so unaccountably, may well be attributed to Cain by those who accept as history the first chapters of Genesis, from which we infer that the earliest

Adamites possessed a full knowledge of much which was lost sight of for long centuries, and only painfully relearned in later times. As Dr. Kitto writes:

> "'To dress and keep' the Garden of Eden, Adam not only required the necessary implements, but also the knowledge of operations for insuring future produce, the use of water and the various trainings of the plants and trees."

Dr. Kitto asks how Adam could have done the work appointed for him without iron instruments:

> "Iron cannot be brought into a serviceable state without processes and instruments which it seems impossible to imagine could have been first possessed except in the way of supernatural communication. . . . *To make iron* (as is the technical term) requires previous iron. . . . Tubal Cain most probably lived before the death of Adam; and he acquired fame as 'a hammerer, a universal workman in brass and iron.' Genesis iv, 22.)" (Kitto's *Cyclopædia.* Adam.)

We gather therefore, that Tubal Cain's ancestor Cain may have taken the knowledge of arts and crafts into Babylonia. The tempter had told Eve that the Fruit of the Tree of Knowledge would make her and Adam as "gods"; what limit, therefore, can be put to their capabilities? Discoveries witness to the fact that the culture of Babylonia in Sargon's time was of a very high order, and that the art of that period excelled all later art. No adequate explanation for this fact can be found unless we believe that Sargon was Cain, and had inherited the miraculous knowledge of his parents.

Referring to the perfection of the earliest works of Babylonian art, which he ascribes to the reign of Sargon, Professor Kittel says that they

> "lay the axe to the dogma of a continuous and unbroken line of evolution,"

and that they far excel any of the later Babylonian art and also that of the early Greek period. Describing some Babylonian works he says:

" The surprising delicacy of execution, the noble beauty and fidelity to nature by which these representations are characterised, must excite the rapture of everyone who sees them ; they would, in my judgment, do honour to the atelier of a Begas or a Dondorf . . . they come down to us from the time of Sargon I and therefore belong, at the latest, to the fourth, perhaps even to the fifth millennium before Christ.   The material of these figures, as determined by a thorough chemical examination, consists of an alloy of copper and antimony." (*Babylonian Excavations, etc.*, p. 22.)

How, the Professor asks, can we account for the existence of this beautiful art in earliest Babylonia and how can we explain the fact that a

" degradation must have taken place—a species of intellectual impoverishment—a retrograde movement, and a falling off from a previous higher stage of culture."   (P. 23.)

In my opinion, this beautiful and realistic art was introduced by Cain, and the question of its degradation will be discussed later. Unfortunately, the British Museum possesses no example (so far as I know) of the true art described by Professor Kittel —all that we find there is in the usual hieratic mock-archaic style.

VIII

ANOTHER indication of the identity of Cain with the Babylonian Sargon is that the name variously rendered Sargon, Sargoni, Sarrukinu, Shargani, etc., may reasonably be taken as synonymous with " King Cain,"[1] the first syllable Sar or Shar meaning ruler or King in Babylonia[2] and obviously the origin of Shah, Czar, Sahib, Sire, Sir, etc., while the second syllable gon, gani, gina or kinu, is very like Cain. George Smith writes :

> " Several of the other names of antediluvian patriarchs correspond with Babylonian words and roots, such as Cain with gina and kinu."[1] (*Chaldean Genesis*, p. 295. Early edition.)

[1] *Times History*, Vol. I, p. 373. " Shar-kishati means king of the world."
[2] *Altaic Hieroglyphics*, p. 59. Conder.
According to Professor Waddell, the English language is based upon Babylonian. (*Phœnician Origin of Britons*. 1926.)

IX

SARGON'S DATE

WE also, it seems, have the right to believe that Sargon's date, circa 3,800 B.C. agrees with Cain's. Accepting Archbishop Ussher's reckoning, which has never been discredited, Adam was created about the year 4,004 B.C. and he is said to have lived 930 years. Cain may have been born soon after 4,004 B.C. and may, like Adam's other descendants before the Flood, have lived many hundreds of years (according to Jewish tradition he lived 730 years[1]). That Sargon lived long is indicated by the tales of his marvellous exploits and travels. It seems necessary indeed to picture the Babylonian king as endowed with longevity; and this would account for "the enormous gaps" in Babylonian history which Assyriologists fill up with admittedly conjectural kings and even dynasties.

The great ages of the Biblical patriarchs are sometimes treated as fabulous, but the words in the sixth chapter of Genesis—"Yet his days shall be an hundred and twenty years"—seem to imply that human life was to be curtailed, and while there is no evidence that men did not live to the great ages mentioned in the Bible, the whole weight of tradition tends to show that they did.

The gods and demi-gods of the Egyptians were said by the priests to have lived many hundreds of years; and to adopt Professor Kittel's line of argument, would they have imagined that longevity if it had never existed? Although the Jews are known to have disputed as to whether it was common to all men to live to a great age[2] in those times, they never questioned the longevity of the patriarchs.

Josephus (38 A.D.) gives a list of ancient authorities who held

[1] *Biblical Antiquities of Philo*, p. 78. Trans. by M. R. James. L.D. 1917.
[2] Kitto's *Cyclopædia of Biblical Literature*. Longevity.

that "the ancients" lived nearly a thousand years,[1] and suggests a commonsense reason for those long lives, saying :

> " And besides, God afforded them a longer time of life on account of their virtue, and the good use they made of it in astronomical and geometrical discoveries, which would not have afforded the time of foretelling the period of the stars unless they had lived 600 years ; for the Great Year is completed in that interval."

In answer to an enquiry at the British Museum the Secretary wrote (quoting Mr. A. C. D. Crommelin of the Astronomer Royal's staff at Greenwich) : " It appears that the 600-year period alluded to by Josephus consists of two of the most satisfactory cycles, that is 300 years, for the calculation of total eclipses. How the ancient astronomers became aware of these cycles seems to be unknown." This ancient knowledge can therefore only be accounted for in the way that Josephus suggests or as direct revelation.

Another reason for the longevity of the patriarchs is suggested by a writer who points out that Adam lived with Methuselah for about 233 years, that Methuselah died in the year of the Deluge, and that, therefore,

> " there was only one person needed—the godly Methusaleh—to transmit the Sacred Hebrew Records from Adam, the First Father of Mankind, to Noah the Second Father of Mankind. And thus is illustrated one purpose for which a few godly lives were so prodigiously prolonged before the Deluge." (*The Origins of the Bible*. Rev. A. B. Grimaldi.)

The Chinese, too, have accounts of primeval longevity in their records. One writer says :

> " It is a curious circumstance that the Emperor Ho-ang-ti who, by the chronology of China, must have been contemporary with the patriarch Reu [Abraham's great-great grandfather], when the life of man was shortened to about three hundred years,

---

[1] *Josephus*. Antiquities. Book I. Chap. 3. Part 9.

proposed an enquiry in a medical book of which he was the author, whence it happened that the lives of their forefathers were so long compared with the lives of the then present generation." (*Prefaet. ad Sin. Chron. Couplet*, p. 5.)

Finally, a Babylonian list of kings has lately been found in which the reigns of the kings are almost exactly the same length as the lives of Adam and his descendants. Adam, for example, lived 930 years (Genesis v), while the first king in the list is said to have reigned 900 years. Seth lived 912 years, while King Zugagib lived 940 years. Enos lived 905 years, while Etana reigned 635 years, and the eighth king is said to have reigned 1,200 years, thus outdoing Methuselah, who only lived 969 years.[1]

What explanation can there be for the remarkable resemblance between the duration of the reigns of the Babylonian kings and that of the lives of the Bible patriarchs, unless it be that one list was copied from the other, or, still more likely, that they are independent records of the same personages. My own conviction is that the so-called " dynastic list " is simply a disguised reference to the ages of the earliest Biblical characters—that the different names given to these kings were invented by the priests and that there are no grounds for concluding, as some writers have done, that this list of Babylonian kings is older than the Bible records.

One reason for this opinion is that in this list the fifth king (Etana) is said to have been translated to Heaven, which seems like an echo of the Bible story of Enoch ; and another is that the twelfth king Enmerkar is said to have built the city of Erech " with the people of Erech "[2] which, if Professor Sayce is right in identifying Erech with Enoch, is an obvious allusion to Cain's building of that city.[3] Professor King saw a connection between Cain and Enmerkar, although he does not identify them, for he writes :

" Cain's city-building, for example, may pair with that of Enmerkar." (*Legends of Babylon*, p. 38.)

[1] *Legends of Babylonia*, p. 24. L. King.
[2] *Legends of Babylon, Egypt, etc.*, p. 35. L. King.
[3] See p. 27.

Believing that Cain (i.e. Sargon) built Erech, I naturally accept
Colonel Conder's opinion that Sargon was the first king of
Erech,[1] and reject Dr. Hall's opinion that Sargon conquered a
former king of Erech[2] called Lugal-Zaggisi. Colonel Conder
thinks that Lugal-Zaggisi meant " the Great Lord (or king)
Sargina " and that both names were applied to Sargon, while
Professor King shows how the same achievements are ascribed
in the inscriptions to Sargon and Lugal-Zaggisi and evidently
suspected the accuracy of the accounts of the latters exploits,
on one page he wrote :

> " It is true that Shar-gani-sharri of Akkad, at a
> rather later period, did succeed in establishing an
> empire of this extent, but there are difficulties in the
> way of crediting Lugal-Zaggisi with a like achieve-
> ment." (*Sumer and Akkad*, p. 198.)

Writing several years later than Dr. Hall, who takes Shar-
gani-sharri and Sargon to be two different kings,[3] Professor
King gives reasons for the conclusion that they are the same
person.[4] This confusion arises (I claim) from the fact that
the Babylonians wilfully twisted and distorted the history
recorded in the Book of Genesis, and more evidence of this
will be given later.

The importance of this " king-list " from my point of view
is that it shows that the longevity of the Bible patriarchs was
known of in Babylonia, which helps to verify the statements in
Genesis, and may persuade the sceptical to accept the probability that Cain was alive in the year 3800 B.C., the date
ascribed to Sargon, and for centuries after. Considering that
no Egyptian king can be dated with any certainty previous
to the Ptolemaic period (about 500 B.C.) it is a striking fact and,
to my mind, providential, that this very early date should have
been established. Professor Sayce describes how, against his
previous judgments, he was forced to accept the evidence that

[1] *The First Bible*, pp. 217-218.
[2] *The Ancient History of the Near East*, p. 185.
[3] *The First Bible*, pp. 217-218.
[3] *The Ancient History of the Near East*, p. 186.
[4] *Sumer and Akkad*, p. 221.
[4] And see Appendix D.

Sargon of Akkad lived as early as the fourth millennium before Christ, and says how that fact " shook to its very foundations " his previous theories.   He tells how

> " the last king of Babylonia, Nabonidas, had anti-quarian tastes, and busied himself not only with the restoration of the old temples of his country, but also with the disinterment of the memorial cylinders which their builders and restorers had buried beneath their foundations. It was known that the great temple of the Sun-god at Sippara, where the mounds of Abu Habba now mark its remains, had originally been erected by Naram-Sin the son of Sargon, and attempts had been already made to find the records which, it was assumed, he had entombed under its angles. With true antiquarian zeal, Nabonidas continued the search . . . until . . . he had lighted upon ' the foundation-stone ' of Naram-Sin himself. This ' foundation--stone ' he tells us had been seen by none of his predecessors for 3200 years. In the opinion, accordingly, of Nabonidas, a king who was curious about the past history of his country, and whose royal position gave him the best possible opportunities for learning all that could be known about it, Naram-Sin and his father Sargon I lived 3200 years before his own time, or 3750 B.C." (*Hibbert Lectures*, 1887, p. 21.)

The American excavator, H. V. Hilprecht, writes :

> " Nabonidas, the last Chaldean ruler of Babylon, succeeded in bringing to light the foundation-stone of Naram-Sin, the son of Sargon of Agade, which for 3000 years no previous king had seen, conveying to us by this statement the startling news that this great ancient monarch lived about 3790 B.C., a date fully corroborated by my own excavations at Nuffar." (*Excavations in Assyria and Babylon*, p. 273.)

X

SARGON'S MONUMENTAL DATE DISPUTED

SINCE these views were expressed Assyriologists have seen fit to throw doubt upon this early date, and the news which startled Professor Hilprecht is discarded by them. Prof. King explains that to accept this date as accurate entails the leaving of " enormous gaps in Babylonian history which the invention of kings and even dynasties has not succeeded in filling up."[1] These gaps can, I contend, be accounted for by my theory that Cain reigned in Babylonia many hundreds of years and was probably followed by an equally long-lived son, since Naram-Sin seems to have been almost as famous as his father and to have made even more extensive conquests.

Other Assyriologists, in endeavouring to compile a consecutive history of ancient Babylonia, choose to discard Sargon's date, 3800 B.C. In the latest edition of the *British Museum Catalogue* we find (pp. 4-5) :

> " It is now generally thought that the scribes of Nabonidas either made a mistake in copying or that there was a mistake in the architype ; in fact, that they wrote 3200 instead of 2200. We may assume then that Sargon reigned between 3000 B.C. and 2700 B.C."[2]

[1] *Sumer and Akkad*, p, 61. L. King. It seems noteworthy that Professor King, who, in this work, published elaborate lists of Sumarian kings, should thus confess their conjectural character.

[2] The reluctance to accept Sargon's early date leads to some confusion. Professor Waddell, for instance, in a footnote, says " the founder of the 1st Sumer dynasty about 3100 B.C. who uses the swastika and figures himself as a Fire-priest, often records his presentation of a ' Font-pan ' or ' Font of the Abyss ' . . . to different temples which he erected. . . . Sargon I, about 2800 B.C., as high-priest who uses the swastika, describes himself as ' water-libator ' and devotee Nu-iz-sir (=Nazir) of God." (*Phœnician Origin of Britons*, p. 273. 1925.) How much simpler to regard both kings as one and the same.

It is fortunate that this rather confusing statement which clashes with my theory, is only guesswork.

It seems strange that Sargon's date should be so lightly discredited to make way for mythological lists of kings with unconvincing names. In the *Times History* we read:

> " Unfortunately, these ancient lists consist, for the most part, of tables of names having strange and unfamiliar sounds. To the average reader these names are necessarily repellent. Such words as E-anna-tum, Urumush or Alusharshid, Samsu-iluna, Kadashman-Karbe cannot well be otherwise than mystifying when unconnected with any vivid sequence of tangible events. And for the most part the names of these earliest rulers of Babylonia stand in the present state of our knowledge, as mere names, with only here and there a suggestion of tangibility. . . . The present knowledge does not by any means suffice to give us a full list of the names of these early monarchs. . . . Whatever is written to-day regarding early Babylonian history must then, in the nature of the case, be subject to possible revision to-morrow. . . . Meantime, we must be content with the glimpses into here and there an epoch, and with the citation of here and there a name, covering as best we may some three or four thousand years of Babylonian history in a few meagre chapters." (Pp. 349-350.)

Since this was written one or two writers have boldly, on the strength of these scattered names, composed so-called histories of ancient Babylonia ; but a close examination shows that no satisfactory records exist of the period of history between Sargon of Akkad and his son, and the reign of Hammurabi, who is regarded as the Amraphael of Genesis xiv, 1, the contemporary of Abraham.

The long list of imaginary kings has all the air of being authentic ; but I agree with the writers[1] who claim that some of those names (Lugal-Kigub and Lugal-Zaggisi, for instance) are only other titles for Sargon. The fact that those kings are credited in inscriptions with the very same achievements as

[1] *Worship of the Dead*, p. 400. Garnier.

Sargon justifies this conclusion. I go further and suggest that most of the names in these lists were mere inventions of the Babylonian priests[1] which are now used to fill up the "enormous gaps" in history caused by the immensely long reigns of Sargon (Cain) and his son. As a leading anthropologist remarked in 1875:

> "There are huge gaps in our knowledge of the history of the human race, and it has been the pleasure of mankind in all ages to people these gaps with jugglers and bogies." (Col. Lane Fox, President of the Anthropoligical Institute, May 28th, 1875.)

The royalties foisted upon us by the Babylonian priests resemble "bogies" more than human beings; as an example of this the portrait of Ur-Nina King of Lagash with his sons is reproduced, facing p. 23.

A recent writer, commenting upon the arbitrary rejection of Sargon's date as attested to by Nabonidas, says that it

> "involves the very serious step of scrapping a positive statement made by a king who stood nearly 2500 years nearer than we do to the events which he was dating, and whose scribes had doubtless had access to documents which carried them back very much further still." (*The Life of the Ancient East*, p. 107. J. Blaikie. 1923.)

Naturally, since Sargon's date agrees with my theory about Cain, I gladly accept it. It seems strange that Assyriologists have ignored the possibility of any connection between Sargon and Cain in spite of the illuminating facts that Sargon reigned when, according to the Bible, Cain may have been alive, that the name Sargon means King Cain, and that the Babylonian "Erech" was probably the city Enoch built by Cain. It is especially strange that Professor Sayce, who tacitly admits Cain's historical reality by suggesting that he built that city, should overlook the possibilities entailed by that suggestion. Cain was born and bred in the atmosphere of the miraculous; his parents were possessed of supernatural knowledge, some of

[1] See Appendix D.

which must have been imparted to their children, they had been designed for immortality and, to judge by their longevity, some spark of that immortality must have survived in their descendants for many centuries. Cain's presence, therefore, would offer the most reasonable key to the problem of ancient Babylonia.

The story of the Tree of Knowledge is now often regarded as a kind of fairy tale, founded upon Babylonian legends and unworthy of serious consideration; but this view is strongly opposed by the fact that (as we shall see later) the conception of the Tree of Knowledge found its way into Babylonia before 2000 B.C. together with other details of the Bible story, while the nonsensical and paradoxical references to that story in the Babylonian inscriptions cannot reasonably be taken as anything but the wilfully corrupted form of the events described in the Bible.

Even some thinkers who accept the miracles of the New Testament doubt those recounted in the Old. Dr. Charles Gore, former Bishop of Oxford, writes:

> "The Christian religion could not have begun without miracles or the belief in miracles, so I think that to-day we are rationally led to believe that they actually occurred, and that without such belief the conviction of the Christian faith would not hold its ground."

Yet for the first chapters of Genesis he has little use, probably because of the miraculous element in them. According to him

> "we should regard Adam and Eve not as historical individuals, but as Man and Woman—as Everyman."
> (*Can We Believe?* Canon Gore.)

Is it not equally rational to believe that the Hebrew religion began with the miraculous events recorded in Genesis, and that without those events there would have been no religion at all? Christianity, as Saint Augustine (of Hippo) remarked, began in Genesis and, judging by the way in which the pioneers of Christianity refer to the Book of Genesis, his sentiment was inspired by their writings. Is it reasonable, therefore, to draw the line between the miracles of the Old and New Testament ?

Just as the true religion required miracles as a foundation, so, I suggest, did also the false religion of Babylonia, which we shall look into later ; and this would account for the obscure allusions in the Babylonian mythological inscriptions to the miraculous events described in the first chapters of Genesis.

XI

AN IMPROBABLE THEORY

BEFORE bringing forward evidence from the Babylonian inscriptions in further support of my theory of the identity of Cain with Sargon, the site (to continue my former metaphor) must be cleared to facilitate the building up of that theory. With the reader's help (for his whole attention is wanted here) the most formidable obstruction must now be dealt with, for we come up against the theory held by most Assyriologists that the ancient civilisation of Babylonia, which I ascribe to Cain, was evolved by an inferior race called Sumerians or Akkadians who, according to Professor Sayce, were probably blacks.[1]

From their study of the monuments Assyriologists infer that Babylonia was first inhabited by two races, one being an inferior type, and the other a superior white race, which they think eventually ruled over the inferior one. But, and this is the weak part of the story, they hold that it was the inferior race which evolved the astonishing civilisation and culture of ancient Babylonia, the art of cuneiform writing and the mythology, all of which was absorbed (they tell us) by the conquering race which ruled the land as early as the third millennium before Christ, and who became the powerful Babylonians mentioned in the Bible.

It is therefore to this inferior race that the invention of the mythological account of the Creation is ascribed and it is their gods which are supposed to be the models from which were " borrowed " the characters described in the first chapters of Genesis.

Even Assyriologists who accept this story see its weakness. Professor Sayce says :

[1] See footnote, p. 17.

" This is so startling, so contrary to preconceived ideas, that it was long refused credence by the leading orientalists of Europe . . . even to-day there are scholars, and notably one, who has himself achieved success in Assyrian research, who still refuse to believe that Babylonian civilisation was originally the Creation of a race which has long since fallen into the rear rank of human progress." (*Ancient History*.)

Professor King who also held this theory, admits that the monuments testify to the presence of both races in Babylonia at the beginning of history ; he writes :

" It would thus appear that at the earliest period of which remains or records have been recovered, Semites and Sumerians were both settled in Baby-lonia." (*Sumer and Akkad*, p. 53.)

in which case it is surely to the superior race that we should look for the originators of the civilisation and culture. Naturally, since this authority regards the inferior race as the pioneers of the Babylonian civilisation, he believes that the oldest gods first belonged to that race and were taken over in later times by the superior race who conquered them. While holding this opinion himself he frankly admits that at least one authority argued against it, because in the monumental drawings those gods are represented as members of the superior race, and says :

" Man forms his god in his own image, and it is surprising that the gods of the Sumerians should not have been of the Sumerian type." (*Sumer and Akkad*, p. 49.) (See illustrations facing p. 149.)

So shadowy are the grounds upon which are based this improbable theory, that some Assyriologists doubt the existence in Babylonia of any other race than the so-called Semitic race to which Sargon belonged. Sir James Frazer writes :

" Assyriologists are by no means agreed as to the occupation of Babylonia by an alien race before the arrival of the Semites."

It suits my theory, however, to believe that a race different from the so-called Semitic race to which Sargon belonged lived first in Babylonia.   I regard those people as the pre-Adamites over whom Cain ruled and the fact that all accounts of them are of the slightest description seems to me natural, for if they were an inferior race, as we should infer from the Bible and the monuments, they would have left no records of any kind.   Any names or actions attributed to them were, therefore, probably invented by the later historians of Babylonia.   As one writer says :

> " We are constrained to view the Sumerians solely in the light of their successors." (*Times History*, Vol. I, p. 461.)

XII

THE SUMERIAN PROBLEM

IT seems that the reasons why the inferior race is supposed by Assyriologists to have evolved the ancient civilisation of Babylonia are first, that Sargon in whose reign that civilisation existed, could not in their opinion have originated it, since its evolution must have required many centuries; a very natural conclusion since they do not identify Sargon with Cain; and secondly, that most of the inscriptions upon the monuments are written in a mixed dialect, very different from the Babylonian language talked by Sargon and later Babylonians. Because of the primitive style of the larger part of the inscriptions most scholars believe that their language was that of the inferior race who, they therefore claim, originated the civilisation of Babylonia, as well as the cuneiform writing.

Since this opinion is irreconcilable with my own that it was Sargon (King Cain) who introduced that civilisation and culture, I must, before further attempting to build up my theory, try to put before the reader as concisely as possible both sides of the question. Fortunately, a school of Assyriologists exists whose views unintentionally support my own. That school is called "Halévyan" after the French Assyriologist Joseph Halévy, while the opposing school is known as "Sumerian."

This question is known as "The Sumerian Problem," and in studying it, it must be remembered that the word "Sumerian" is applied to the people whom I regard as pre-Adamites, and the word "Semite" to Sargon and his race. This problem is said to be "of vital importance" to those who wish to know more about the history of Ancient Babylonia. A supporter of the "Sumerian school" writes:

"After a long dispute carried on chiefly by philologists it is now generally conceded that the earliest civilisation of Southern Babylonia was due to a non-Semitic people, the Sumerians.   To this people it would seem, must be ascribed the honour of developing the chief features of Mesopotamian civilisation, including the invention of the cuneiform system of writing. (*Ency. Brit.*, Ed. XI. Sumer.)

The Halévyan school, on the other hand, considers that the language of the inscriptions is merely an invention of the Babylonian priests of later times and represents

> " nothing more than a priestly system of cryptography based of course upon the common phonetic speech." (*Times History*, Vol. I, p. 310.)

In Professor Halévy's opinion the earliest characters from which grew the cuneiform writing testify to the Semitic origin of that writing and completely

> " refute the hypothesis of early decipherers that there existed on Babylonian soil prior to the Semites an alien race called Sumerians, or Akkadians, from whom came the cuneiform characters as well as the entire Semitic civilisation of Babylonia." (*Times History*, Vol. I, p. 310.)

This opinion has been supported by Professor Delitzsch, and other German critics, and agrees with Professor Hugo Winckler's statement that the Babylonian inscriptions exhibit the same characteristics as the monk's latin and as the Macaronic compositions, though he says:

> " in the latter case the linguistic hybridations are often humorously meant and this mongrel Sumerian is always serious." (*History of Babylonia and Assyria*, p. 14.)

To give some idea of what, in the above writer's opinion, the Sumerian language is like, I quote the *Century Dictionary*, which describes the Macaronic writing as

> " characterised by the use of many strange, distorted,

or foreign words or forms, with little regard to syntax, yet with sufficient analogy to common words and constructions to be or seem intelligible."

The " philological dispute " is therefore this : the Sumerian school claims that an inferior race called Sumerians invented the writing, etc., of Babylonia, which the superior race called Semites afterwards absorbed ; on the other hand, the Halévyan school denies the existence of the inferior race altogether, and claims for the superior race the invention of the Babylonian writing, civilisation and culture. A means of reconciling these opposing views is offered by my theory that the inferior language is that of the pre-Adamites, whose existence we infer from the Bible, that the superior language was that of Cain, and that the two languages were mixed up by the scribes of later days into a kind of secret dialect.

XIII

PROFESSOR LEONARD KING'S ULTIMATUM QUESTIONED

BECAUSE of the apparently primitive language in which most of the inscriptions are written, certain versions of the Creation, Fall of Man, and the Deluge, are believed by the Sumerian school to date back to the time before Sargon of Akkad, to be the work of the " Sumerians," and to be the models on which both the Bible and Babylonian stories were founded. As we have seen, this opinion has been disputed; but in 1916 Professor King announced his conviction that the controversy must be settled in favour of the Sumerian school, since quantities of tablets had been found at Nippur in Babylonia, which were almost entirely written in the " Sumerian " language.

This hardly justifies his conclusion, however, if as another Assyriologist writes :

> " Nothing found at Nippur can be dated with any certainty earlier than 2500 B.C." (*Religion of Babylonia and Assyria*, p. 595. M. Jastrow.)

For in that case the " Semites " who are known to have been in Babylonia before that date may have already invented the " priestly cryptogram " which Professor Halévy believes the " Sumerian language " to be. Professor King seems to discount his own conclusion and to support that of Professor Halévy by saying that hundreds of the Babylonian tablets are inscribed with " grammatical compilations," and lists of Sumerian words accompanied by their translations into the Babylonian speech, which, he says, shows how carefully the primitive Sumerian language was studied by the Babylonian priests. He writes :

> " The late Sir Henry Rawlinson rightly concludes that these strange texts were written in the language

of some race who had inhabited Babylonia before the Semites, while he explains the lists of words as early dictionaries compiled by the Assyrian scribes to help them in their studies of this ancient tongue." (*Sumer and Akkad*, p. 4.)

According to Professor Jastrow:

> " Many of these school texts were written in a Sumerian version, though emanating from priests who spoke Babylonian."   (*Religions of Babylon and Assyria*, p. 279.)

It seems evident that the scribes, who thus studied the primitive language with apparently a view to resuscitate it, could put as much or as little of it into their inscriptions as they chose, and that these comparatively newly discovered inscriptions may have been their latest productions instead of the work of the ancient inhabitants of Babylonia.

Professor Sayce, although sharing in the opinion that the Bible and Babylonian stories were originated by the " Sumerians," admits that those stories have come down to us through generations of Babylonian priests. He writes in reference to the Sumerian story of the Creation :

> " Its antiquity is shown by the fact that it is written in the ancient language of Sumer . . . but it is evident that the old poem has been revised and re-edited by the priesthood of Babylon . . . the Creator-god Ea has been supplanted by Merodach . . . it is possible that even in its alterations at the hands of theologians of Babylon the old cosmological poem of Eridu has been modified in accordance with the requirements of a theology which resulted from a fusion of Sumerian and Semitic ideas." (*Religion of the Babylonians*, p. 379.)

It seems strange that the Professor, who sees the artificiality of this story, can feel convinced of its " Sumerian " authorship. To me it is only one of the corrupt versions of the Creation story handed down from the time of Cain by the Babylonian priests. It is indeed a recommendation for the Halévyan theory, and incidentally for mine as well, that if either of them is adopted, the supposed Sumerian inscriptions may be regarded as nothing more than the nonsensical inventions of the pagan priests, and probably part of a scheme to mystify posterity.

XIV

SUGGESTED RECONCILIATION OF THE TWO THEORIES

IF only, as before suggested, the Sumerian school would accept the Halévyan theory that the language of the inscriptions is a concoction of the priests ; and if in return the Halévyans would accept the theory of the Sumerian school that the inferior dialect is a real language, as I am inclined to regard it, their views could be reconciled and would fit in with my own that the superior language was that of Cain[1] and the inferior that of the pre-Adamites. Such a mutual concession would not be incompatible with the science of philology. After carefully discussing both sides of the question, an American professor writes :

> " The Semitic priests and scribes played with and on the Sumerian idioms, and turned what was originally an agglutinative language into what has almost justified Halévy and his followers in calling Sumerian a cryptogram." (J. Dyneley Prince, Prof. of Semitic Languages, Columbia University. *Ency. Brit.*, Ed. II. Sumer.)

His further remarks show that he would willingly agree with the Halévyan school that the language of the inscriptions was an arrangement of the priests for purposes of mystification, were it not for the fact that he cannot satisfy himself that the inferior part of the language was not a real language once spoken in Babylonia. Since he cannot satisfy himself on this point he practically gives up the problem.

It can hardly be denied that if my theory about Cain and the pre-Adamites is accepted it solves the " Sumerian problem," and since " the evidence of a theory increases with the number

---

[1] As we have seen, the language of Sargon resembled Hebrew. See p. 22.

of facts which it explains " there is much to be said in its favour.

For my purpose it matters little whether the inferior language of the Babylonian inscriptions belonged to the pre-Adamites or was invented by the priests. That question I leave to philologists. What does matter to me is the discovery made by both schools that the writers of the inscriptions chose to mix that inferior language with their own, for by doing this they make their writings almost unintelligible, thus supporting my theory that they wilfully obscured their meaning.

XV

THE GREAT CONSPIRACY

> Babylon hath been a golden cup in the Lord's hand,
> that made all the earth drunken : the nations have
> drunken of her wine ; therefore the nations are mad.
> Jer. xl, 7.

HAVING done my best to satisfy the reader that there is no proof that the Babylonian civilisation and culture were evolved by an inferior race, the ground is cleared for the further building up of my theory that Cain was identical with Sargon, and that to his superhuman knowledge of good and evil must be attributed the ancient glory of Babylonia as well as her enduring shame.

Discarding the teaching of the Sumerian school that the inferior race of Babylonia gradually evolved (presumably from sticks and stones) the earliest gods and goddesses, it seems natural to regard Cain as their inventor ; for as Professor Kittel argues, the idea of false deities can only have occurred in the first instance to one who possessed the knowledge of God. And since, as I show later, the oldest gods Anu and Isthar represent Adam and Eve, the fact that they were first worshipped in Erech or Unuk (the city probably built by Cain)[1] points to this conclusion.

> " There are some reasons for believing that the oldest seat, and possibly the original seat, of the Anu cult was in Erech as it is there where the Isthar cult . . . took its rise." (*Ency. Brit.*, Ed. XI, p. 113.)

as does also Professor Sayce's statement that an astro-theology grew up in the court of Sargon in which the heavens, etc., were

[1] See above, p. 27.

divided between Anu, Ea and Bel, whom I regard as representing Adam, Eve and the Devil.[1]

If Cain was Sargon, St. John's statement that he was " of that wicked one "[2] finds striking support in the Babylonian inscriptions in which Sargon is called the son of the Devil, as in the following :

> " The divine Sargani, the illustrious king, a son of Bel the just, the king of Agade and of the children of Bel." (*The First Bible*, Colonel Conder, p. 220.)

Bel, the " Lord of the underworld," is called alternately in the inscriptions Mul-lil and En-lil, and Sargon's allegiance to the Devil under the latter name is alluded to in an inscription upon a votive vase of white calcite stalagmite as follows :

> " To the god Enlil the king of all lands, king Sargina king of Erech, the world-king, the prince of God, the mighty man, the obedient son of the god Ea . . . the great ruler or patesi[3] of the divine king of all lands, listening obediently to the god Enlil . . . having become sole chief of Erech, invoking Nina the far-famed lady of Erech ; through the mighty aid of his god, in the day that the god Enlil made to king Sargina the grant of royalty on earth, allotted to him in sight of the world, the hosts of the lands being obedient from east to west, he has added every land by making conquest. . . . He has made the high place of Erech a shrine of Ea?" (*The First Bible*, Colonel Conder, p. 219.)

Evidence will be given later that the names Nina and Ea both represent Eve (or Isthar). Colonel Conder gives another inscription purporting to be of Sargon :

> " King Sargina, king of Erech, having overthrown the world . . . has erected a temple this day for the god Enlil, king of all lands, to worship Enlil, king of all lands, all his life long. . . . Let the world's eye henceforth behold the favoured place, prosperity enduring for many years." (P. 218.)

[1] *Hibbert Lectures*, 1887, pp. 400-402.
[2] St. John iii, 12.
[3] " Priest-king (patesi)." *Cambridge History*, Vol. I, p. 148.

CYLINDER WITH EIGHT FIGURES   [See p. 55.

Reproduced from King's "A History of Sumer and Akkad," by permission of the
Publishers, Messrs. Chatto and Windus.

[Face p. 55.

If these words are not meant as a tribute to the " prince of this world " through the medium of King Cain, it is difficult to imagine any meaning in them. Further reasons will be given for believing that Cain was the human originator of idolatry, but its instigator must have been " the Prince of Darkness." What greater insult than the worship of false gods could have been offered to the Creator by the disgraced Spirit and the outcast man ? As Robert Browning wrote :

> " Note that the climax and the crown of things
> Invariably is—the Devil appears himself—
> Armed, accoutred, horns and hoofs and tail."

And sure enough those baneful signs are inseparable from the Babylonian religion ; for in their drawings all their gods and heroes are represented with horns or hoofs or tail.[1] (See illustration.)

Thus, I dare to think, sprang up a great conspiracy cunningly devised to catch the souls of men. Mankind had already forfeited the immortality of the body, but their souls were still free to soar. Once caught, their souls were to be drugged and maddened with the wine of the Golden Cup until soul, as well as body, had forfeited eternal life.

The New Testament gives a lurid picture of Cain's followers ; and the monuments amply testify that the Babylonian priests who were, if my theory holds good, the first of those followers, deserved the denunciations hurled at them by the Apostle Jude :

> " Woe unto them. For they have gone in the way of Cain, . . . these are the spots in your feasts of charity, when they feast with you, feeding themselves without fear ; clouds they are without water, carried about of winds ; trees whose fruit withereth, without fruit, twice dead, plucked up by the roots ; raging waves of the sea foaming out their own shame ; wandering stars, to whom is reserved the blackness of darkness for ever."

---

[1] The Moon-god Sin, confused in inscriptions with En-lil or Bel, is called " The Uplifter of Horns." (*Hibbert Lectures*, 1887, p. 128.)

XVI

THE BABYLONIAN PRIESTS

ONE fact, little commented upon in modern works on ancient Babylonia and Egypt, is the tremendous power possessed by the priests who were responsible for the inscriptions. Yet to my mind, unless we appreciate the full significance of this fact, we cannot hope to unravel the intricacies of the historical material left behind by them. It is not always realised that the literature and art of those countries were entirely in their hands for at least 2,000 years before Christ; and that they could therefore hand down as much or as little of their history as they chose.

Speaking of the Babylonian inscriptions, Professor Maurice Jastrow says:

> "It was through the temple schools and for the temple schools that the literature which is wholly religious in its character, or touches religion at some point was produced . . . the functions of the priests were differentiated, and assigned to several classes . . . diviners, exorcisers, astrologists, physicians, scribes and judges of the court to name only the more important . . . the power thus lodged in the priests of Babylonia and Assyria was enormous. They virtually held in their hands the life and death of the people." (*Religion of Babylonia and Assyria.* M. Jastrow, Professor of Semitic Languages, University of Pennsylvania.)

These all-powerful priests were the hereditary conspirators, the custodians of the Golden Cup—the legacy of Cain. They, as we have seen, are known to have possessed from the time of Sargon a language resembling Hebrew, and the art of cuneiform writing, and could therefore have left behind them a clear and detailed history ; instead of which, they left confused and almost undecipherable inscriptions written in a mongrel dialect. What but a desire to mystify could have prompted such apparent stupidity, or the following equally irrational custom adopted by them and described by Professor Jastrow :

> " The inscriptions upon the bricks found in the library of Assurbani-pal were copies of very much older writings collected from all parts of Babylonia belonging to a great literary movement which took place in the time of Khammurabi (circa 2000 B.C.) when the prevailing myths, religion and science of the day were embodied in numerous works ; and the later Assyrians and Babylonians were content to copy these writings instead of making new work for themselves." (*Religion of Babylonia and Assyria.*)

What but my theory can explain why the scribes of Assurbani-pal's reign devoted their time and energy to copying earlier works referring to past events and characters ? If, as I contend, Cain armed with superhuman knowledge and power, came into Babylonia bringing with him the marvellous story of the Creation of the world and the Garden of Eden, how tame by comparison must the later history of Babylonia have seemed, and how insignificant its later monarchs. No wonder the old times were perpetually harped upon in inscriptions in which are veiled allusions to Adam and Eve—the Fall of Adam—Eve's sorrow for Abel and her anger against Cain—the coming of Cain to Babylonia and his alliance with the Devil.

These illusions are cloaked in the form of mythology which originated (as I hope to show) in Cain's travesty of the truth in transferring the Divine attributes of the Creator to three false gods, whom he called Anu and Ea, after his parents, and Bel, after the Devil.

The monotheistic inscriptions to be produced later, prove that the knowledge of the One God had reached Babylonia at the beginning of history, and St. Paul says that, although " from the Creation of the World," God had made Himself

E

known to men, they had corrupted that knowledge into idolatry :

> " Professing themselves to be wise, they became fools, and changed the glory of the uncorruptible God into an image made like to corruptible man, and to birds, and fourfooted beasts, and creeping things. (Romans i, 22-23.)

The evil character of the priests is betrayed by their inscriptions which show that they practised cannibalism. Professor Sayce says : " Human flesh was consumed in Babylonia in the earliest times in honour of the gods," and " human sacrifices were part of their religion."[1]

Although, as one writer says, " the conception of the soul had been arrived at in the age of Sargon of Akkad,"[2] the doctrines taught by the priests were in the last degree materialistic. The soul of man was said to be in the liver, and every sheep's liver contained (it was taught) the liver of a god, and was an instrument of divination, etc. Hundreds of brick models of livers have been dug up, also directions showing the meaning attached to different diseases and deformities of the liver.

The inscriptions, which prove that the knowledge of One God and His Laws existed in Babylonia in the earliest times,[3] make it evident that the degrading teaching of the priests was an outcome of evil and not of ignorance. Just as the later Babylonian art shows, as Professor Kittel remarks, " a falling off " from that of Sargon's time (suggesting a wilful degredation) and just as the use of a " mongrel dialect " by the priests in place of their actual language shows a wilful degradation of literature as well as a desire to mystify, so the substitution of innumerable gods for the One God can only indicate a wilful suppression of the truth. The strongest evidence of the priests' duplicity is met with in examining the Babylonian myths, and three of these may be mentioned here. They cannot have escaped the notice of the first Higher Critics, and therefore seem to justify Professor Kittel's statement that they did not

---

[1] *Hibbert Lectures*, 1887, p. 83. Appendix E.
[2] *Religion of Babylonia and Assyria.* Prof. Jastrow.
[3] These monotheistic inscriptions are quoted later.

necessarily believe that the Bible stories were borrowed from Babylonian myths, but invented that theory to popularise Assyriology. George Smith says that :

> "the dark race is called Admi or Adami which is exactly the name given to the first man in Genesis," and "it appears from the fragments that it was the race of Adam or the black race which was believed to have fallen." (*Chaldean Genesis*, p. 9.)

If, as some Higher Critics hold, an Israelitish scribe invented a history of his race with the help of Babylonian literature, would he have chosen the name of the black race in Babylonia for his primeval ancestor? Is it not more likely that the Babylonian priests applied the name of the first white man to the black race as part of their conspiracy of lies—a very masterpiece of mockery. It seems obvious too that the Babylonians were intentionally misrepresenting the sequence of the events in the story of the Creation, when they said that the Moon was created before the Sun.[1] And is it possible to imagine that the Bible story of Eve's creation was inspired by the Babylonian one of the first woman's creation by " seven evil spirits " of whom it is said that

> " The woman from the loins of the man they bring forth." (Sayce, *Hibbert Lectures*, p. 395.)

Could anyone honestly believe that the Genesis story of Eve's temptation and loss of immortality was inspired by the Babylonian story of the serpent that deprived a hero of a plant capable of rejuvenating and keeping men alive.[2] The resemblance between the two stories seems to me to show that one is the parody of events described in the other, for it is obvious that they both had the same origin.

Professor Pinches, discussing the Babylonian literature, says :

> " There is hardly any doubt that a desire existed to make things as difficult as possible. . . ." (*Ancient Egypt*, Part 3, 1923. Editor, Prof. Sir Flinders Petrie.)

[1] In the Babylonian Creation story.
[2] *Ency. Brit.* Ed. II. Serpent—worship.

Another scholar comments upon the universal system of obscurantism practised by pagan priests :

> " This dominant priesthood, whose domain was knowledge, holding the keys of treasured learning, opened the lock with chary hands, and veiled plain speech in fantastic allegory. In such allegory Egyptian priests spoke to Greek travellers who came to them as Dervish pilgrims or Wanderlande students. It was this sybilline knowledge that an Aeschylus, an Ovid, or a Virgil, master of wizards, here and there revealed. It is this dragon-guarded treasure of secret wisdom that we may yet seek to interpret from graven emblem, from symbolic monuments, from the orientation of temple walls, from the difficult interpretations of non-Hellenic names of hero and heroine ; god and lunar goddess, of mysterious monster and fabled bird, of celestial river and starry hill ; names that were first written in the ancient language of a people wiser and more ancient than the Greeks." (Professor Darcy W. Thompson, *Transactions of the Royal Society of Edinburgh*, Vol. I, Part I, No. 3.)

The " treasured learning," veiled in fantastic allegory was, I shall try to show, the knowledge of God and of the events and characters recorded in the first chapters of Genesis, all of which became less and less recognisable as the centuries rolled on.

In case the discovery that the blacks of Babylonia were called Adami should by any possibility be thought to support Sir James Frazer's theory that the story of Adam originated among the African tribes and that Adam was a black man, it would be well to call attention to a drawing in which Adam and Eve, though far from beautiful, are undoubtedly represented as white people.   (See illustration facing.)

George Smith writes :

> " One striking and important specimen of early type in the British Museum collection has two figures sitting one on each side of a tree, holding out their hands to the fruit, while at the back of one is stretched

ADAM, EVE AND THE SERPENT

See p. 60.

CHERUBIMS IN BABYLONIAN
ART

See p. 69.

TAKING THE HAND OF
BEL

See p. 99.

The above three illustrations are reproduced, by permission, from " Chaldean Genesis," by G. Smith, published by Messrs. Sampson Low, Marston and Co. Ltd.

[Face p. 60.

a serpent. We know well that in the earliest sculp-
tures none of these figures were chance devices, but
all represented events or supposed events and figures
in their legends; thus it is evident that a form of
the story of the Fall similar to that of Genesis was
known in early times in Babylonia." (*Chaldean
Genesis*, p. 55.)

XVII

THE ORIGIN OF MYTHOLOGY

In dealing with mythology—"that fantastic allegory"—another difficulty confronts me. My views upon this subject differ from those held by many well-known and influential writers, and therefore, before showing that the Babylonian mythology provides the surest signs of the identity of Cain with Sargon, I must examine those opposing views. So admired and renowned are their exponents that only my conviction of their fallacies lends me courage to oppose them.

It is, as Max Muller says :

> " the silly, savage and senseless element that makes mythology the puzzle which men have so long found it." (*Ency. Brit.*, Ed. II. Mythology.)

and this element is just what one would expect to find in it, if it is nothing more or less than the result of Cain's determination to counteract the worship of God so faithfully preserved by the other branch of Adam's race.

From the days of ancient Greece learned men have puzzled over the unnatural features of mythology and the mystery of its origin, and at least five different explanations had been offered for it before the Birth of Christ. They were the physical explanation of Theagenes, the religious or theosophic explanation of Porphyry, the explanation of the myths as allegories; Aristotle's opinion that the myths were the inventions of legislators " to persuade the many and to be used in support of the law," and finally the view propounded by Euemerus (316 B.C.), according to whom the myths were history in disguise and :

" all gods were once men whose real feats have been decorated and distorted by later fancy." (*Ency. Brit.*, Ed. II. Mythology.)

Needless to say, this is the view with which my theories agree, and it agrees with St. Paul's words.[1] Did not the pagans by attributing God-like qualities to men, change " the uncorruptible God into an image made like to corruptible man " ? Although the writer of the following passage pins his own faith to a more modern view he admits that there is much to be said for the explanation offered by Euemerus ; he writes :

" This view suited Lactantius, St. Augustine and other early Christian writers very well. They were pleased to believe that Euemerus ' by historical research had ascertained that the gods were once but mortal men.' Precisely the same convenient line was ·taken by Sahagun in his account of Mexican religious myths. As there can be no doubt that the ghosts of dead men have been worshipped in many lands, and as the gods of many faiths are tricked out with attributes derived from Ancestor-worship, the system of Euemerus retains some measure of plausibility. While we need not believe with Euemerus and with Herbert Spencer that the god of Greece or the god of the Hottentots was once a man, we cannot deny that the myths of both these gods have passed through and been coloured by the imaginations of men who practised the worship of real ancestors. For example, the Cretans showed the tomb of Zeus, and the Phœnicians (Pausanias X, 5) daily poured blood of victims into the tomb of a hero, obviously by way of feeding his ghost . . . very probably portions of the legends of real men have been attracted into the mythical accounts of gods of another character, and this is the element of truth at the bottom of Euemerism." (*Ency. Brit.*, Ed. II Mythology.)

This authority (Andrew Lang) like other modern mythologians prefers the latest explanation of mythology, which is

[1] See p. 58.

that it gradually evolved from the imagination of primitive man.   He writes :

> " Our theory is therefore that the savage and senseless element in mythology is, for the most part, a legacy from the ancestors of the civilised races who were in an intellectual state not higher than that of Australians, Bushmen, Red Indians, the lower races of South America, Mincopies and worse than barbaric peoples.   As the ancestors of the Greeks . .   advanced in civilisation their religious thought was shocked and surprised by myths (originally dating from the period of savagery, and natural in that period) which were preserved down to the time of Pausanias by local priesthoods, or were stereotyped in the ancient poems of Hesiod and Homer, or in the Brahmanas and Vedas of India, or were retained in the popular religion of Egypt." (*Ency. Brit.*, Ed. II. Mythology.)

If the Greeks had really been shocked by ancient myths we might agree with this writer in regarding these myths as peculiar to a state of ignorance, but since the Greeks themselves not only adopted the ancient mythology of Babylonia,[1] but added to it some even worse features, it was obviously the outcome not of ignorance, but of evil, powerful enough to resist the vaunted evolution of civilisation.   Professor Max Muller says about the Greek mythologians :

> " they would relate of their gods what would make the most savage of Red Indians creep and shudder . . . stories, that is, of the cannibalism of Demeter, of the mutilation of Uranus, the cannibalism of Cronus, who swallowed his own children, and the like.   Among the lowest tribes of Africa and America we hardly find anything more hideous and revolting." (*Ency. Brit.*, Ed. II. Mythology.)

If, too, we glance at Roman mythology, which it is now recognised owed its origin through the Greeks to Babylonia, could any custom be more barbarous than that still carried on near Rome in Imperial times, namely the constantly

[1] See footnote, p. 108.

recurring murders of the priest-kings of Nemi, about which Sir James Frazer writes :

> " The strange rule of this priesthood has no parallel in classical antiquity and cannot be explained from it. To find the explanation we must go further afield . . . no one will probably deny that such a custom savours of barbarous days and, surviving into imperial times, stands out in striking isolation from the polished society of the day, like a primeval rock rising from a smooth shady lawn." (*Golden Bough.*)

May it not be further back, rather than " further afield " that we must look for the origin of this custom ? Sir James Frazer has searched the world over for its explanation and has failed to find it, but does not the story of Cain, granted that he was the Babylonian king Sargon, provide the most reasonable explanation of this ancient custom in which murderers, masquer·· ading as kings and priests, were honoured ? However this may be, the important fact remains that one of the most barbarous of customs survived at that late period of history in an outwardly polished society, because beneath the surface lurked the besotting influence of the Golden Cup of Babylonia.

In my opinion, the theory that Cain, inspired by hatred and revenge, invented false gods is manifestly more probable than the theory that a system, which has held men's imagination throughout the whole history of the world, was devised in the first place by ignorant savages. If, as Professors Kittel and Max Muller claim, it is psychologically impossible that the notion of gods can have preceded the knowledge of the One God, where can we look for the originator of the gods of Ancient Babylonia if not to Cain ? And how can we reasonably account for the existence of so " silly, savage and senseless " a system as mythology, except as being the corrupted stream of " ancient knowledge revealed by God to man " ?

Just as " Shadow owes its birth to light," so mythology owes its existence to the truth, for as everything combines to show, it is nothing more than its distorted shadow. Like the clinging weed which devastates a cornfield, mythology has, I hold, obscured the whole of ancient history.

XVIII

EUEMERUS SUPPORTED BY OTHER WRITERS

IT will be seen therefore, that the view propounded by Euemerus harmonises with my own theory of the system of obscurantism practised from earliest times by the Babylonian priests; and it can scarcely be denied that in his time evidence in favour of his theory may have existed of which nothing is now known. The American Assyriologist Albert Clay (one of the latest writers upon the subject) says:

> "The fact that Euhemerism, as it was developed, was in time completely disregarded, does not prove that Euhemerus was wrong. As far as I can ascertain, since the excavations at Troy, and in the light of other discoveries, not a few classical scholars hold that many of the so-called Greek and Roman gods were heroic personages." (*The Origin of Biblical Traditions*, p. 27.)

Augustine, the African Bishop (A.D. 354-430) in his book *De civita Dei*, says:

> "Alexander the Great told his mother in a letter that even the higher gods . . . were men, and the secret was told him by Leo the high priest of Egyptian sacred things . . . Alexander requested his mother to burn the letter in which he said this." (*Worship of the Dead*, p. 15, Garnier.)

The outstanding feature of mythology is its bewildering variations, its " kaleidoscopic interchange of gods and goddesses," as Professor Sayce describes it, which I contend was meant to blind posterity to the fact that, under the baffling verbiage of the priests' writings, historical events and characters were hidden.

For this purpose the names, sexes and relationships of the mythological characters seem to have been changed in different periods and places; father and son are hopelessly confused, as are also mother, sister and wife. Many of the deities have both male and female forms. In Babylonian mythology, for instance, Anatu the wife or consort of Anu is generally a form of Anu, and she is also one of the many forms of the goddess called Isthar.[1] While the first Babylonian god Anu evidently represents Adam, the chief god of the Hindus is also Adam, for one of his names is Adama and his wife is called Iva. One writer points out that Noah is represented in Indian mythology by the god Menu, whose sons, first called Sama, Chama and Pra Japeti and later on Brahma, Siva and Chrishna were unmistakably the representatives of Shem, Ham and Japhet, because, as he says:

> " They are described as the children of one who was preserved in an ark with seven companions."
> (*Origin of Pagan Idolatry*, Vol. 2, p. 102, Faber.)

We are thus encouraged by many writers to look upon the mythological characters as the deified forms of the first men and women, although that view is not popular with modern scholars.

[1] *Hibbert Lectures*, 1887, p. 184. Sayce.

XIX

THE ROOT OF MYTHOLOGY

THE Babylonian gods are the first of which we have any monumental record. In studying them, therefore, we are as it were, getting down to the root of mythology and analysing the ingredients of the Golden Cup of Babylonia, which, down through the ages, has blinded the majority of mankind to the truth.

Having, I hope, convinced the reader of the improbability of the "black heads" having evolved the civilisation of Babylonia, and that on the contrary it was invented by the great Sargon, who, as Professor King says, was "the actual founder of his dynasty";[1] it follows that we may also attribute the institution of the oldest known gods to Sargon (namely Cain), and this furnishes a very reasonable explanation of how the mythological systems of the world first came into being.

Although the connection between those gods and the Bible characters is admitted by some Assyriologists, they regard the former as the prototype of the latter, whereas I claim that it was Cain (the "high-priest of Enlil"), and after him generations of priests who travestied the miraculous story of the Garden of Eden; although, since that story dwarfed everything in their experience, it is perpetually harped upon in their so-called religious writings.

Professor King, who held that the Babylonian myths were adopted by the Hebrews, says :

> " The association of winged guardians with the sacred tree in Babylonian art is at least suggestive of the cherubims and the tree of life."

[1] *Sumer and Akkad*, p. 232.

And in discussing the resemblances between the Hebrew and Biblical writings he says :

> " We come then to the question, at what periods and by what process did the Hebrews become acquainted with Babylonian ideas ? " (*Legends of Babylonia*, pp. 136-141.)

To that question Professor King suggests four alternative answers, but arrives at no conclusion. It does not seem to have occurred to him that the Hebrew and Babylonian stories were (as Professor Kittel believes) independent versions of the same original, although from every point of view it seems to be the reasonable solution of the problem.

Presumably influenced by opinions such as Professor King's, some theologians have relinquished their faith in the miraculous character of the Genesis stories and regard them as inspired by the Babylonian myths. They credit some unknown Israelitish scribe with the authorship of the Book of Genesis, and attribute the ethical teaching of that Book to the influence exerted upon the author by the later prophets (circa 700 B.C.).[1] But is it conceivable that so spiritually-minded a writer (under such influence) should have invented a fictitious story of the origin of his race, adopting two Babylonian gods as its first parents, or that he took his idea of the Tree of Life from such drawings as the above ?[2]

[1] *The Doctrine of the Infallible Book*, p. 14. Canon Gore.
[2] See illustration facing p. 60.

XX

THE BABYLONIAN GODS AND GODDESSES

" The examination of names is the beginning of learning." (Socrates.)

Assyriologists believe that a literary revival took place in Babylonia about 2000 B.C., when all the ancient traditions of that country were collected and written down; and if, as certain facts seem to prove, Cain settled in Babylonia about 1800 years before that date, those traditions, full of references to Biblical characters and events, are easily accounted for. They, I hold, are nothing less than the corrupted version of the ancient history recorded in the first chapters of the Bible.

Most of the examples I quote are taken from translations given by Professor Sayce. They are dull and tiresome reading, because of their contradictions and absurdities, but for my purpose it is of course necessary to examine them. The Professor tells us that the first Babylonian gods were a trio—" the supreme gods Anu, Mul-lil and Ea," and that there was a fourth god called Tammuz. These four gods seem to be regarded by Assyriologists as the models from which Adam, Eve, the Devil and Abel were drawn, but my contention is that, on the contrary, they were the deified representatives of those Bible characters, and that it was Cain who deified their memories by transferring to them some of the attributes of God. This contention finds support in the notable fact that Cain himself had no place in that oldest group of gods.[1] Had he not been its inventor he would surely have been included in it, a fit companion for Bel the Devil.

Professor Sayce says about the fourth god Tammuz, whom he calls the prototype of Abel :

" The primitive home of Tammuz had been in

[1] As we shall see, Sargon was deified in later times.

that Garden of Eden or Edin which Babylonian tradition placed in the immediate vicinity of Eridu,[1] hence his mother (and wife) is called 'the lady of Edin'." (*Hibbert Lectures*, p. 23.)

He also says that like Abel, Tammuz was a shepherd and was killed when young.[2]

Assyriologists suggest that the Biblical " Garden of Eden " was so-named after some locality in Babylonia, but my suggestion is that the Babylonian Eden or Eridu (as it is sometimes called) more probably took its name from the original garden which Cain had known of in his youth, and that the name was brought into " The Land of Nod " by him.

Professor Sayce seems to identify the second god of the great trio with Satan by writing :

> " The supreme Bel was Mul-lil who was called the god of the lower world, his messengers were nightmares and demons of the night, and from whom came the plagues that oppressed mankind." (*Hibbert Lectures*, p. 147.)

Another writer says :

> " Mul-lil was the original Bel of the Babylonian mythology and was lord of the surface of the earth and of the affairs of men."[3] (*Chaldean Genesis*, G. Smith, p. 58.)

Having identified these two gods with Abel and Satan, it is obvious that Anu and Ea (or Isthar) must have represented Adam and Eve.

Professor Sayce says that :

> " the city of Erech was the seat of the gods Anu and Isthar who were afterwards adopted by the Hebrews."

and as they certainly did not adopt them as gods this must mean that he regards them as the prototypes of Adam and Eve.

[1] " It was at Eridu that the Garden of the Babylonian Eden was placed." (*Religion of the Babylonians*, p. 263.)

[2] *Hibbert Lectures*, p. 245.

[3] The Devil is described three times by our Lord as the Prince of this world. John xii, 31 ; xiv, 30 ; xvi, 11.

It is noticeable that while in later mythology gods were never by any chance reduced to the status of men, Anu, if he had really been the model from which Adam was drawn, must have been divested by the supposed writer of Genesis of the highest estate ever attributed to a pagan god ; and Isthar must have been reduced from her position as " Queen of Heaven," to that of a mere woman.   They, with the god Tammuz, would have been the only exceptions to an otherwise invariable rule of the mythological system.

About the god Anu, George Smith writes :

> " At the head of Babylonian mythology stands a deity who was sometimes identified with the heavens, sometimes considered as the ruler and god of heaven. This deity is named Anu, his sign is the simple star, the symbol of divinity, and at other times the Maltese cross. Anu represents abstract divinity, and he appears as an original principle, perhaps as the original principle of nature." (*Chaldean Genesis*, p. 54.)

Anu is called in one inscription " the king of angels and spirits, lord of the city of Erech."[1]   In another, " Anu the chief, the father of the gods."[2]   The temple of Erech (Enoch) was called " the house of Anu," and " the house of heaven." Anu is also called " the lord of the old city," meaning Erech,[3] otherwise called Unuk).

The glorification of Anu left no place in Babylonian mythology for a Supreme Being, although, as we shall see, the existence of God was known from the earliest historical times in Babylonia.   Anu's only rivals in mythology were Bel, to

---

[1] *Chaldean Genesis*, p. 53.

[2] *Legends of Babylonia and Egypt*, p. 109.   L. King.

[3] *Chaldean Genesis*, p. 55.   The name " old city " applied to Erech seems consistent with the theory that that city was built by Cain, for his city would naturally have been the oldest in Babylonia ; and another name for Erech— " the place of the settlement "—is also appropriate if Cain first settled there. (*Hibbert Lectures*, p. 185.)   Professor Sayce says that the name of " Unuk is found on the oldest bricks " and is " the same as Enoch built by Cain." (Index *Hibbert Lectures*.)

" The capital of this part of the country was Uruk, called in Genesis Erech. Erech was devoted to the worship of Anu, the god of heaven, and his wife, the goddess Anatu, as well as of Istar, the Phœnician Ashtoreth, or Astarte, the myth of whose love for the Sun-god Dumuzi or Tammuz, the Adonis of the Greek story, is alluded to in the course of the poem," i.e. the Epic of Gizhubar. (*Chaldean Genesis*, p. 192.   1880.)

whom his titles as well as his wife are sometimes transferred,[1] and Marduk, who in later Babylonian mythology inherited, Bel's and also Anu's designations. Usually Anu is described as the god of heaven, Bel as that of the earth, and Ea or Enki of the waters. In the Babylonian story of the Creation of the World we find the lines :

> " Isthar with Anu the king into a noble seat they raised and in the government of heaven they fixed."
> (*Chaldean Genesis*, p. 109.)

This is, I suggest, a veiled reference to Cain's deification of Adam and Eve ; and the inscription in which Anu and Isthar are called the lord and lady of the holy mound[2] is probably an allusion to the Garden of Eden. In a curious myth translated by Professor Sayce, the Tree of Life (or perhaps that of Knowledge) is surely referred to in connection with Anu, Ea and Bel :

> " The altars amid the waters, the treasures of Anu, Bel and Ea, the tablets of the gods, the delivering of the oracle of heaven and earth, and the cedar-tree the beloved of the great gods, which their hand has caused to grow." (*Hibbert Lectures*, p. 241.)

Again the Tree of Life may be meant by " the mighty plant of Anu which Ea, the divine antelope, carried to a place of purity."[3]

The third member of the trio of gods is Ea, who Professor Jastrow says was the god of water :

> " the third in a great triad, of which the other two members were Anu, the god of heaven, and Bel the god of earth." (*Religion of Babylonia and Assyria*.)

Here again I find myself at loggerheads with the professors who regard Ea as distinct from Isthar, while in my opinion they both represent Eve. Their reason being presumably that Ea is a male god, while Isthar is nearly always represented as a goddess, but the fact that, although Isthar is often Anu's

---

[1] One of Isthar's titles as wife of Bel was Belit-ili or Innana. *Legends of Babylonia*, p. 63.
[2] *Hibbert Lectures*, p. 113.
[3] *Hibbert Lectures*, p. 530.

F

partner, Ea is the third in the first triad of gods in which the two others represent Adam and the Devil, leaves no doubt in my mind that Ea as well as Isthar represented Eve. Unless we realise the priests' system of obscurantism we cannot make head or tail of their writings.

Other reasons for regarding Isthar and Ea as one and the same are that they are both described as parents of Tammuz, the mythological representative of Abel, and are both associated with the serpent ;[1] and it could scarcely be a mere coincidence that while Anu is connected in the inscriptions with both Isthar and Ea, Adam's wife is called in the Bible both Ishar "Woman in Hebrew" and Eve

Isthar is usually represented as " the Great Mother," the Dea Myrionymus or goddess of ten thousand names who, Professor Sayce tells us, was represented by all the Babylonian goddesses and most of the later Egyptian, Greek and Latin ones ; and who is obviously the deified form of Eve, for among her many names she is called " Mother of Mankind,"[2] " the Lady of Eden,"[3] " the Beloved of Anu",[4] " the Goddess of Birth,"[5] " the Goddess of the Tree of Life,"[6] " the Lady of Rising,"[7] etc.

Under the name of Nina or Nintu [8] Isthar is said to have divined all the mysteries of the gods—surely a reference to Eve's acquisition of God-like knowledge described in the Bible. Professor King says :

> " Nina . . . who could divine all the mysteries of the gods." (*Sumer and Akkad*, p. 266.)

And the next lines can only refer to Eve's remorse at sight of the terrible results of her disobedience :

> " Isthar cried aloud like a woman in travail, the Lady of the gods lamented with a loud voice (saying) :

[1] *Hibbert Lectures*, pp. 282-283.
[2] *Legends of Babylonia and Egypt*, p. 64. L. King.
[3] *Hibbert Lectures*, 1887, p. 336. Sayce.
[4] *Hibbert Lectures*, 1887, p. 531. Sayce.
[5] *Legends of Babylonia and Egypt*, p. 112. L. King.
[6] *Hibbert Lectures*.
[7] *Hibbert Lectures*, p. 259.
[8] " It is pretty clear that Nina, ' the lady,' must have been the primitive Istar . . ." (*Hibbert Lectures*, p. 282.)

The old race of man hath been turned back into clay, because I assented to an evil thing in the council of the gods, and agreed to a storm which hath destroyed my people that which I brought forth." (King, *Babylonia Religion*, p. 134.)

It is consistent with my theory of the identity of Isthar with Ea that Ea was, according to Professor Sayce, regarded in Babylonia as " the author of knowledge and intelligence,"[1] and was called " the God of Culture."[2]

Professor Jastrow remarks that no god shows such distinct proof of having been submitted to " theological changes as Ea," but does not suggest, as I do, that Ea represented Eve.

It seems reasonable, however, to think that Ea, although a male god, represented Eve, since Isthar is sometimes turned into a male deity ; Professor Sayce speaks of :

" the doubt as to whether Isthar were male or female." (*Hibbert Lectures*, p. 254.)

and mentions an astronomical tablet in which she is a female at sunset and a male at sunrise.   (P. 254.)

In a curious " bilingual hymn " Ea is evidently referred to as " the mighty mother " ; and allusions are also made to Eridu or Eden, to Tammuz (Abel) and to the tree in the midst of Eden.   Some of the words are :

" In Eridu a stalk grew . . . in a holy place did it become green . . . (before) Ea was its course in Eridu, teeming with fertility . . . (there is the home) of the mighty mother who passes across the sky. (In) the midst of it was Tammuz." (*Hibbert Lectures*, p. 238.)

In another cryptic writing the name of Ea is said to be recorded upon " the core of the cedar tree " which was thought to " shatter the power of the incubus," and to cure people

---

[1] *Hibbert Lectures*, p. 118.
[2] *Hibbert Lectures*, p. 136.

possessed by devils.[1]   While another inscription connects Ea
with Eden by saying :

> " The divine bulls of Ea and his wife were named
> the god of the field of Eden and the god of the
> house of Eden." (*Hibbert Lectures*, p. 289.)

Then to confuse matters further Ea's wife Davkina is
said to be the mother of Tammuz, Professor Sayce remarks :

> " As mother of Tammuz, Davkina the wife of Ea,
> had a special name. . . . As she seems to be identified
> with Istar in the same passage, we may conclude
> that the compiler of the mythological list regarded
> her as equally the mother and the wife of Tammuz."
> (*Hibbert Lectures*, p. 237.)

If Ea and Isthar (otherwise Dav-kina) represented Eve, as
I believe they do, the priests excel themselves here by making
Eve her own wife.

Although he does not suggest that Ea and Isthar were
different forms of the same deity Professor Sayce notices some
connection between the two ; he says that Isthar was also
Yasmu " the wise one," the " Lady of the Deep," " the Mistress
of the Abode of the Fish," and " the Voice of the Deep," and
that, therefore, she must have ranked with Ea the Fish-god and
" Lord of the Deep."[1]   And at least one student of mythology
supports my contention that Isthar and Ea were identical by
saying : " Istar the ocean-mother and female form of Ia."[3]

The legend of Isthar's descent into Hell to bring back Tammuz (Abel) is evidently, as Professor Sayce points out, the
origin of the later legends of Isis and Osiris, of Demeter and
Persephone and of Eurydice and Orpheus, and according to the
same authority Isthar became the Ashtoreth of the Canaanites,
the Astarte of the Phœnicians, as well as Diana or Artemis,
Venus or Aphrodite.

Isthar's relationship to Tammuz is varied in the Inscriptions,
but in whatever form, period or country, the Great Mother

---

[1] *Western Asiatic Inscriptions.* 11.59-10-11. " Eridu, the seat of the
Chaldean god of culture, Ea, whose home was in the deep." Sayce, *Religion
of the Babylonians*, p. 262.

[2] *Hibbert Lectures*, 1887, p. 111.

[3] *The Ruling Races of Prehistoric Times.* J. F. Hewitt.

is represented in mythology, she is accompanied by a young hero who has some tragic end. Professor Sayce writes:

> " When the legend of Tammuz got to Greece his mother was said to be his sister." (*Hibbert Lectures*.)[1]

As Anatu, Isthar was the wife of Anu, although as Isthar she is sometimes called his daughter, while at other times she is said to be the daughter of Sin the Moon-god; Professor Jastrow says:

> "Isthar, it will be observed, is here called the daughter of the Moon-god, whereas in the Gilgames Epic she appears as the daughter of Anu, the god of heaven." (*Religion of Babylonia and Assyria*, p. 566.)

Professor Sayce writes:

> " Belit the wife of Bel is sometimes identified with Isthar, as Belit she is called 'the lady of lands, dwelling in Enmash-mash'." (*Hibbert Lectures*, p. 237.)

In obscure inscriptions like those in which Ea is mentioned, and in the constant interchange of the names and attributes of the gods and goddesses we see what Max Muller calls the " silly and senseless " element in mythology, and they fully justify Professor Pinches' opinion[2] that the priests intended their writings to be as unintelligible as possible.

The savage element in mythology to which Max Muller also alludes is shown by Professor Sayce's description of the rites and ceremonies practised in the worship of the goddess Isthar, first at Erech and afterwards in other Babylonian cities. At Erech, he says:

> " Unspeakable abominations were practised in the name of Isthar which were outdone in horror in other Babylonian cities. The black Isthar, as we may call her, was the parody of the goddess of love and the rites with which she was adored and the ministers by whom she was served were equally parodies of the cult which was carried on at Erech. Her priestesses were the witches who plied their unholy calling under the shadow of the night and mixed the poisonous

---

[1] *Cambridge History*, Vol. I, p. 413. Tammuz, son of Innini. Ditto, p. 404. Innini identified with Isthar. p. 442. " Tammuz and his sister Ishtar."
[2] See p. 59.

philtres which drained away the strength of their hapless victims." (*Religions of Ancient Egypt and Babylonia*, pp. 342-343.)

It is strange that Professor Sayce, who sees that the priests parodied the earlier cults of Isthar, seems to have no suspicion that the whole system of mythology with all its absurdities and contradictions is, as it were, a parody of the truth and that its myths and mysteries were in fact, as Sir William Ramsay writes: "elaborate and artificial products of a diseased religion."[1] On the contrary, the Professor holds, as we have seen, that the Bible stories were founded upon the Babylonian mythology.

[1] *Times Literary Supplement*, September 17th, 1925.

XXI

CAIN THE SUN-GOD MERODACH OR MARDUK

> " It is by the patient accumulation of apparently trifling facts that the most important generalisations are achieved." (Deville's *Prolegomena*.)

ALTHOUGH we do not find among the oldest Babylonian gods one of which Cain could have been the prototype, we certainly find him in later mythology. He could not well have deified himself, but his followers would naturally have honoured his memory in that way after his death. The monuments show that Sargon was deified,[1] and the words " Sargon is my god " are found in a few inscriptions, but it is (in my opinion) the most celebrated of all the Babylonian gods, Merodach the sun-god, who was Sargon's real representative in mythology. To Professor Sayce's unanswered question " Now, who was this Merodach, this patron god of Babylon?"[2] my answer is, therefore, the mythological representative of Sargon (Cain); and certainly the name Merodach would have well suited the rebellious Cain if, as one writer suggests, it was derived from marad, to rebel.[3]

It is interesting to note that the Jews spoke of Cain as " the first free-thinker,"[4] It may have been, as Lord Byron suggests, that Cain was the only one of the first few Adamites to rebel against the sentence of death pronounced upon all mankind. (*Cain, a Mystery*.)

One reason for thinking that Merodach represented Cain is that he was the patron-god of Babylon, which city the inscriptions show existed in Sargon's time:

" The Omens place the founding of the city Agade

[1] *Times History*, Vol. I, p. 362. *Cambridge History*, Vol. I, p. 409.
[2] *Hibbert Lectures*, p. 92.
[3] One Vol. *Bible Commentary*, p. 17.
[4] One Vol. *Bible Commentary*, p. 1064.

soon after Sargon's first invasion of the west. He took soil from the outer walls of Babylon and consecrated the boundaries of his new capital by tracing its outer walls with the earth of the holy city of Marduk. He made it after the model of Babylon." (*Cambridge History*, Vol. I, p. 407.)

and in the *Encyclopædia Britannica* we read :

" The history of the city of Babylon can now be traced back to the days of Sargon of Agade (before 3000 B.C.), who appears to have given that city its name. There is every reason to assume, therefore, that the cult of Marduk existed already at this early period." (Vol. I, Ed. II, *Marduk*.)

If we rule out the possibility of its having been built by the pre-Adamites, Babylon may have been one of the seven cities attributed to Cain in Jewish traditions.[1]

Nebuchadnezzar calls Merodach in inscriptions " the first-born, the glorious, the first-born of the gods, Merodach the prince,"[2] suitable titles, one would think, for the first-born of Adam's race.

Marduk or Merodach is the most elusive of the Babylonian gods, the recipient of at least fifty names[3] and of most of the attributes given to the first gods Anu, Ea and Bel. But the fact that Merodach is always called the son or the first-born of Ea at once identifies him with Eve's eldest son Cain, if I am right in assuming that the god Ea was the male form of Eve. Here we have an example of the intricate method of mystification employed by the priests ; for not only is Merodach said to be the eldest-born of Ea, but he is also shown to be the eldest-born of Isthar since Davkina, the wife of Ea is another form of Isthar.[4] To crown their inconsistencies, in the story of the Creation, Merodach's father is called, not Ea as elsewhere,

---

[1] *Biblical Antiquities of Philo*, M. R. James. P. 77.
[2] *Hibbert Lectures*, p. 97.
[3] " Asari—always used of Marduk as an epithet only, as in the tablet of the Fifty Names." *Journal of Egyptian Archæology*, 1922, 8.
[4] " Ishtar inherited the attributes of Davkina." *Hibbert Lectures*, p. 264.

but Anu.[1] Since Anu represents Adam, and Ea and Isthar represent Eve, who could Merodach their eldest born have represented but Cain?

In some inscriptions Tammuz also is called the son of Ea and Davkina, and so is shown to be the brother of Merodach as Abel was of Cain: Professor Sayce writes:

> " Tammuz, the son of the River-god Ea." (*Hibbert Lectures*, p. 212.)

Sargon, too, is called the son of Ea, and one inscription in which he is described as such is a good example of the priests' method of obscuring the truth while allowing it to appear, as it were, between the lines. It runs:

> " Sargon, the mighty man, son of the god Ea, prince of the moon-god, begotten of Tammuz and Isthar." (*Worship of the Dead*, Garnier, p. 399.)

The name of Tammuz is evidently introduced in this inscription as a blind, but the priests, by showing that Sargon was the son of both Ea and Isthar, support my view that both those names represented Eve; while the fact that both Sargon and Merodach are called the son of Ea and Ishtar seems to prove that Merodach was the mythological representative of Sargon, and that, if Cain was Sargon, Merodach was Cain's mythological representative.

Had the priests, whose writings show that Merodach and Tammuz were brothers, also shown that Merodach murdered Tammuz it would have been too obvious, that Cain's murder of Abel was referred to; it is not surprising therefore that no hint of such a thing has been found in the inscriptions. At the same time it seems unlikely that so remarkable an episode should have escaped comment, considering how other events recounted in the first chapters of Genesis were repeatedly alluded to. My suggestion is therefore that a double was invented for Merodach—another Sun-god called Adar—and

---

[1] " Marduk is king . . . they bestowed upon him sceptre, throne and pala . . . by his side he slung the net, the gift of his father Anu." *The Story of Creation. The Origin of Bible Tradition.* A. T. Clay. p. 203.
" Anu had placed a club and a bow in the hand of Merodach." (*Hibbert Lectures*, 1887, p. 102.)

that he, instead of Merodach, was said to have murdered Tammuz. Other Babylonian gods had doubles; and Professor Sayce writes:

" In the Shepherd Tabulu however, we have the double of the Shepherd Tammuz himself." (*Hibbert Lectures*, p. 212.)

Since the shepherd Tammuz had a double, the Sun-god Merodach may also have had one, and that that double was the Sun-god Adar seems certain, for we find that Arēs, his representative in Greek mythology was said to have murdered Tammuz; and since the Greek and Roman mythologies are known to have been inspired by that of Babylonia,[1] we may suppose that although no hint of the murder of Abel by Cain has been found in Babylonian inscriptions the story found its way into Greece and Rome.

[1] *Ency. Brit.*, Ed. II. Canis Major.

XXII

ADAR AND ARES CONNECTED WITH CAIN

PROFESSOR SAYCE says :

> " Another title connects Adar with the Arēs of
> Greek mythology, who in the form of the wild boar
> slew the sun-god Tammuz." (*Hibbert Lectures*, p. 153.)

and he connects Adar with Cain by saying that Adar's

> " title ' lord of the date ' . . . the chief fruit of Baby-
> lonia . . . reminds us of Cain, who was ' a tiller of
> the ground '." (*Hibbert Lectures*, p. 153.)

The title " lord of the date " also connects Adar indirectly
with Sargon of Akkad, for the " dates of Akkad " are often
mentioned in inscriptions.[1] As we see later, Merodach is
credited with the irrigation and agriculture of Babylonia,[2]
again suggesting Cain, and hence perhaps the title of " lord
of the date " given to Merodach's double Adar.

If, as Professor Sayce points out, Tammuz was the mythological Abel, Merodach, the brother of Tammuz, evidently
represented Cain ; and if, as the Professor suggests, the Greek
god Arēs who murdered Tammuz was the later form of the
Babylonian god Adar, Adar also represented Cain. We may
therefore assume that Merodach and Adar were identical—that
they both represented Cain—and that anything said about
them in inscriptions is important for that reason. The fact, for
instance, that Adar is said to be a giant, encourages the hypothesis that the first Adamites were of great stature.

[1] See p. 131.
[2] Pp. 86-87.
[2] P. 144.

83

XXIII

MORE LINKS BETWEEN MERODACH AND SARGON

ANOTHER link between Merodach and Sargon is that they are both represented as high priests; Professor Sayce writes:

> "The dignity of high priest in Babylonia was derived from Merodach." (*Hibbert Lectures*, 1887, p. 551.)

and remarks that Sargon is called in inscriptions "the first high priest." (Ditto, p. 26.)

Again, both Sargon and Merodach are said to be law givers; Professor Sayce says that the former is called: "the deviser of constituted law . . . the very wise" (Ditto, p. 28) and that

> "Merodach is called Asari-elim, the mighty prince, the light (of the gods), the director of the laws of Anu (Mul-lil) (and Ea)." (Ditto, p. 284.)

Merodach is probably referred to below as Sar-Ziri, for who but Cain could have been the king of the desert, son of Adam and Eve?

> "Anu and Anatu have a numerous family; among their sons is Sar-Ziri the king of the desert." (*Chaldean Genesis*, p. 55.)

Granted that Merodach represented Cain and that Ea was the female form of Isthar or Eve, the following inscription refers to Cain's indebtedness to his mother for his knowledge:

> "Moreover he, Merodach, possessed all his, Ea's wisdom; 'My child' Ea had said to him, 'What is there that thou knowest not and what could I teach thee? What I know thou knowest also'." (*Mesopotamia*, Delaporte, p. 141.)

In the following passage we find, it seems to me, two different

84

descriptions of Cain, Merodach representing him when under his mother's influence, and Adar representing him in later life under the influence of the Devil.

Professor Sayce writes :

"Adar bears the same relation to Mul-lil that Merodach bears to Ea. Each alike is the son and messenger of the older god. But whereas the errands upon which Merodach is sent are errands of mercy and benevolence, the errands of Adar are those that befit an implacable warrior. He contends not against the powers of darkness, like Merodach, for the father whose orders he obeys is himself the ruler of the powers of darkness. It is against mankind, as in the story of the Deluge, that his arms are directed. He is the solar hero who belongs to the darkness and not to the light." (*Hibbert Lectures,* p. 154.)

If, as I hold, the priests represented Cain as the Sun-god Merodach or Adar, and amused themselves by addressing hymns to him in that guise, the following lines may refer to Cain's irrigation works in Babylonia :

" 1. Who can escape from thy message (piridi or puridi) ?
2. Thy word is the supreme snare which is stretched towards heaven and earth.
3. It turns to the sea, and the sea dreads it.
4. It turns to the marsh, and the marsh mourns.
5. It turns to the channel of the Euphrates, and
6. The word of Merodach disturbs its bed.
7. Oh lord, thou art supreme ! who is there that rivals thee ?
8. O Merodach, among the gods as many as have a name thou art he that coverest them !
(*Hibbert Lectures,* p. 497.)

It also seems possible that the following "litany" refers to Cain's agricultural achievements in Babylonia :

" 17. Incantation—O Merodach, lord of the world . . . prince,

18. strong one, unique, mighty (gitmalu) . . .
19. hero (tizqaru) supreme, who (subjugates) hostility
    . . .
20. forceful, king of . . .
21. Merodach, whose view (paqtu) is (extended over
    the world) . . .
22. vision and seership (?) . . . the glorious one,
23. divine son of the holy mound . . . [Garden of
    Eden ?] (see p. 79).
24. The deluge of the weapon his hand (directs) . . .
30. gladdener (khada) of the corn and the . . . creator
    of the wheat and the barley, renewer of the herd
    . . .[1]

(*Hibbert Lectures*, p. 537.)

It is suggestive, too, that while Cain in the Bible is " a tiller
of the ground " Merodach in the Babylonian Zodiacal scheme
was

" the ploughman of the celestial fields, the Sun-god
who trod his steady path through the heavenly signs
like the patient ox dragging the plough through the
fields below."

(*Hibbert Lectures*, p. 291.)

and that under the title of Asari, Merodach is said to be

" the donor of fruitfulness, the founder of agriculture,
    The creator of grain and plants, who causes the
green herb to spring forth." (Clay, *The Origins of
Biblical Traditions*, p. 211.)

That Cain, i.e. Merodach, brought the knowledge of spiritual
things into Babylonia may be hinted at in the following words :

" (To) Merodach the prince of the gods, the inter-
preter (bar-bar) of the spirits of heaven and (earth)."[2]

Another indication that Cain was represented by the
god Merodach [Marduk] is that while En-lil is one of the
gods who is said in inscriptions to have " committed to

[1] One of the latest discoveries is that wheat was grown in Babylonia in
the earliest historical period. See article in *The Times* newspaper, January
29th, 1927, by S. Langdon, headed " Wheat in 3500 B.C."
[2] *Hibbert Lectures*, 1887, p. 128.

Marduk the rule of all the lands," he is also said to have bestowed Sargon's dominions upon him. Professor King writes:

> " It has long been known that the early Babylonian king Sharru-kin, or Sargon of Akkad, had pressed up the Euphrates to the Mediterranean, and we now have information that he too was fired by the desire for precious wood and metal. . . . We learn that after his complete subjugation of southern Babylonia he turned his attention to the west, and that En-lil gave him the lands ' from the Upper Sea to the Lower Sea,' and from the Mediterranean to the Persian Gulf." (*Legends of Babylon and Egypt*, p. 8.)

To anyone who accepts my view that the god Marduk represented Cain, the following quotation will be interesting as describing some of his activities in Babylonia. Dr. Hall writes:

> " Legends . . . assign to the Babylonian god Marduk the work of reducing the primeval chaos to order by the separation of land from water and the first founding of the homes of men . . . we evidently have here a very vivid recollection of the time when the whole of southern Babylonia was a swamp : the primitive inhabitants were scattered about on various islands which emerged out of the fens, and in these islands, towns arose, just as Ely and Peterborough arose in England under similar circumstances : dykes were heaped up and the shallows were gradually reclaimed, till the demon of the watery chaos Tiamat, finally vanquished, retreated from the land ; Marduk had created the earth and the two great rivers, and, in the words of the legend, ' declared their names to be good '." (*History of the Near East*, p. 175.)

The priests have successfully blurred their picture of the Sun-god, not only by giving him several names (Merodach, Asari, Adar, etc.), but also by introducing two other Sun-gods, Samas and Tammuz, into their writings ; but Samas is known to have been a later conception (probably representing Shem) and Tammuz was, as we have seen, Abel.

If I am right in believing that Sargon (King Cain) was the great Sun-god of Babylonian mythology, the discovery is of no small importance, for all over the world, in pre-historic times, went " culture-heroes," calling themselves Children of the Sun, and organising amazing civilisations for which explorers have been at a loss to account.[1]   Modern researches show the probability that those civilisations originated in either Egypt or Babylonia, and since it is now taught[2] that the first great rulers of Egypt went there from Mesopotamia, it seems reasonable to believe that Babylonia was the fountain head of those civilisations.   Professor Sayce writes :

> " The Pharaonic Egyptians—the Egyptians, that is to say, who embanked the Nile, who transformed the marsh and the desert into cultivated fields, who built the temples and tombs, and left behind them the monuments we associate with Egyptian culture— seem to have come from Asia ; it is probable that their first home was in Babylonia." (*The Religions of Ancient Egypt and Babylonia*, p. 22.)

A more recent writer, looking round for something which might have inspired man in the beginning with the idea of irrigation, argues that its invention more probably took place in Egypt, because while the effect which the flooding of the Nile had upon the Egyptian crops may have inspired the inhabitants with the idea of artificial irrigation, no such lesson would have been taught to the Babylonians by the flooding of their rivers.[3]   He therefore suggests that the art of irrigation first learned in Egypt was taken from there into Babylonia, and regards Egypt as the cradle of civilisation.

Professor Cherry agrees with this and says :

> " Those who inaugurated the irrigation system of

[1] In some far-off lands the Sun-god's name was " Kane." (*The Children of the Sun*. W. J. Perry, p. 167.)
   " Mr. Perry has described at great length and with a wealth of detail the amazing story of the penetration by these ' Children of the Sun ' of nearly the whole world, so that the signs of them are visible in India, in the Malay, in China, Japan and the Pacific Islands and in Central America and Peru (the Incas)." (H. J. Massingham, *Fee, Fi, Fo, Fum*, p. 30.)
[2] By Professors Sayce, Flinders Petrie, Elliot Smith and others.
[3] *The Children of the Sun*, W. J. Perry, p. 429.

Mesopotamia must have proceeded with deliberate intent." (*The Children of the Sun*, W. J. Perry, p. 429.)

That deliberate intent I ascribe to Sargon of Akkad, and as there is really no evidence to show in which of these lands irrigation first existed this supposition is surely warranted in view of the probability that he was Cain.[1] Science supplies no satisfactory explanation of the ancient irrigation of Babylonia and Egypt. All attempts to trace its evolution have been fruitless. Nothing less than the God-like knowledge possessed by Adam and Eve and its transference to their sons can adequately account for it.

A modern novelist makes the philosopher of his imagination say :

> " Wherever agriculture went there went with it traditions of a blood sacrifice, a human sacrifice. I have never been able to imagine satisfactorily why this should have been so ; but very plainly it was so. . . . The Maya, the Aztec religions were insanely bloody." (*World of William Clissold*, H. G. Wells, p. 217.)

The mad wickedness of Cain and his descendants offer, I contend, the most reasonable solution of this problem.[2]

[1] See Appendix F.
[2] See Appendix D, p. iv. Also p. 127.

G

XXIV

ABEL'S MEMORY INSULTED

WHILE Cain, as Merodach, seems to be honoured with such titles as " the redeemer of mankind," " the restorer to life," " the raiser from the dead,"[1] the name Tammuz applied by the priests to Abel was probably intentionally insulting, just as the above titles when applied to Cain (i.e. Sargon) must have been intentionally misleading or ironical, since there is every reason to regard Cain as Satan's staunch ally. If, as I hope to show, the name of Tammuz was an insulting one Professor Sayce's statement that " the name of Tammuz probably grew up in the court of Sargon "[2] acquires a new significance.

Professor Delitszch asserts that the name Tammuz meant " Wahres æchtes kind," and another authority that it meant " lord of life," but Dr. Ball, in a paper of the Society of Biblical Archæology (1894), argues that it really meant a pig and " survives to this day in the Turkish ' domuz,' a hog or pig," and adds :

> " The Chinese presents us with a series of terms for pig in which both elements of the Accadian Domuzi (pig) are evidently found."

This opinion receives involuntary support from Sir James Frazer, who says that Adonis and Attis, who, he tells us, were later forms of Tammuz, were sometimes regarded as boars or pigs, and that :

> " it may be laid down as a rule that an animal which is said to have injured a god was originally the god himself. Perhaps the cry of ' Hyes Attis, Hyes Attis ' which was raised by the worshippers of Attis may be neither more nor less than ' Pig Attis ' ;

[1] *Assyria : its Princes, Priests and People.* Sayce. P. 60.
[2] *Hibbert Lectures*, p. 233.

DEMETER WITH LITTLE PIG   [*See p. 91.*

From antique terra-cotta in possession of Mrs. Robert Yerburgh.

[*Photo : Culbard, Castle Douglas.*

[*Face p. 91.*

Hyes being possibly a Phrygian form of the Greek
' Hyes,' a pig." (*Golden Bough*, 2nd edition, Vol. 2,
p. 22.)[1]

He also remarks that it was :

> " consistent with a hazy state of religious thought
> that the pig should have been held to be an embodi-
> ment of the divine Adonis." (*Golden Bough*, 2nd
> edition, Vol. 2, p. 23.)

The only consistency I can find in this paradoxical arrangement is that in a country where Cain was the " hero of heroes,"
Abel's memory may have been insulted by the undignified
appellation of pig.

That this was the case is shown to be probable by the fact
that although the Babylonian inscriptions do not connect
Isthar (Eve), the mother of Tammuz with a pig, Demeter, her
representative in Grecian mythology, is connected with one.
Demeter was unquestionably a later form of Isthar, for just as
Isthar is said to descend into the under-world to rescue Tammuz,
so Demeter descends into Hades to rescue Persephone—just
as Isthar's departure causes all fertility to cease, so it ceases
upon Demeter's withdrawal into a hiding-place, and just as Ea,
the male form of Isthar, bestows upon mankind through
Merodach, the arts of agriculture, irrigation and law, so in
Greece those arts are attributed to Demeter.

One of Demeter's emblems, a serpent,[2] serves to connect her
with Eve, while another, a little pig, connects her with Abel
(Tammuz).

> " Her attributes are poppies and ears of corn (also
> a symbol of fruitfulness), a basket of fruit and a little
> pig."[2] (See illustration facing.)

And so in classic art we find the mother goddess holding a pig
in her arms—a miniature boar with formidable bristles—the
boar who slew Tammuz and was, therefore, Tammuz himself,[3]

[1] " Thus the monster from whom Andromeda was rescued is merely another
representation of herself." (*The Evolution of the Dragon*, Elliot Smith,
p. 119.)

[2] and [2] *Dictionary of Classical Antiquities*, Nettleship, p. 178.

[3] Professor Sayce says : " Attys was Tammuz " (*Hibbert Lectures*, p. 235),
while Sir J. Frazer connects Attys with Adonis (see p. 103).   George Smith
says " Tammuz became Adonis." (*Chaldean Genesis*, p. 238, 1880.)

Tammuz, the shepherd who lived in Eden, who was killed when young and was loved and mourned by the goddess Isthar, the "Mother of Mankind," and "Lady of Eden." Who but Abel could the pig represent, and who but Eve the goddess?

This is a good example of the grotesque and mocking character of the Babylonian mythology, and of its subtle entry into Europe.

It is surprising that history is being largely evolved from rambling statements about mythological characters in the "Sumerian language," while the historical value of the clearcut stories of Genesis is denied; for as the logician Whateley wrote:

> "The heathen mythology not only is not true, but was not even supported as true; it not only deserves no faith, but it demanded none. The very pretension to truth, the very demand of faith, were characteristic distinctions of Christianity."

At the same time, true history lies hidden between the lines of the Babylonian inscriptions if, as I hold, they are the corrupt version of the events recorded in the Bible. When this view is adopted the "Legend of Sargon," which we shall now examine, becomes full of significance.

XXV

SARGON (KING CAIN) ADOPTED BY AKKI THE DEVIL

IT can hardly be considered a coincidence that while St. John says that Cain was " of that wicked one," referring to the Devil, Sargon is described by the Babylonian priests as being the son or protégé of the Devil. This is one of the strongest indications of the identity of Cain with Sargon, who in different inscriptions is called " the son of Bel the just," " the son of Itti-Bel " and the " son of Dati-Enlil," while Sargon's country is called the " realm of Enlil " (or Bel) who is said to have conferred that realm upon him.

In the " Legend of Sargon " he calls his adopted father " Akki," which is evidently another name for the Devil, for it is closely connected with the name of Nakash the Hebrew serpent—with Ahi, the water-god and serpent—with Ahri-man,[1] who in the Persian religion is the " source of all evil, the devil " —with Agni, the Indian god of fire—with the Egyptian Naka, the serpent—with Naga, the Indian serpent-god—with the Maori demiurge Tiki and with Agu or Acu, another name for the Babylonian moon-god, otherwise called Sin.[2] The moon-god Sin is evidently Bel or En-lil under another name, for in later times the original trio Anu, Ea and Bel became Shamash, Sin and Ishtar (Shamash supplanting Anu, Isthar supplanting Ea, and Sin, Bel.)[3]

The Legend of Sargon, which was discovered and translated by the late Professor Rawlinson in about the year 1867, is said to have been inscribed in its present form in the seventh century

---

[1] Dr. Moffat gives Ahiman as name of giants (Nephilim) in Numbers xiv, 22.

[2] " Ur or Aku, Sin and Itu, in later times generally termed Sin." (*Chaldean Genesis*, G. Smith, p. 55.)

[3] " A second triad was formed of Sin, the moon-god and his two children Shamas and Ishtar, the planet Venus." (*Mesopotamia*, Delaporte, p. 139.)

before Christ. In the *Times History* we find the following translation :

> " Shargina, the powerful king, the king of Agade, am I. My mother was of noble family . . . my father I did not know, whereas the brother of my father inhabited the mountains. My town was Azipiranu, which is situated on the bank of the Euphrates. My mother of noble family (?) . . . conceived me and gave birth to me secretly. She put me into a basket of shurru (reeds ?) and shut up the mouth (?) of it (?) with bitumen ; she cast me into the river, which did not overwhelm (?) me. The river carried me away and brought me to Akki, the drawer of water. Akki . . . took me up in . . . Akki . . . reared me to boyhood. Akki the drawer of water made me a gardener. During my activity as gardener, Isthar loved me . . . years exercised dominion, . . . years I commanded the black-headed people . . . and ruled them, etc."
> (*Times History*, Vol. I, p. 360.)

The legend resembles in some respects the story of Moses, and this is not surprising. The priests of the seventh century before Christ, who are credited with these inscriptions, must have known the early history of Moses and that they should have mixed it up with that of Cain agrees with their usual method of confusing facts. The change of scene from the banks of the Nile to those of the Euphrates is just what might be expected ; while the story of Moses in the ark of bulrushes, rescued by a princess, may have appealed to their dramatic instincts. On the other hand Cain's story is more than hinted at ; his occupation as a gardener—the love of Isthar (or Eve) for him in his youth—his mysterious and sudden arrival in Babylonia—his adoption by the Devil and his long rule over an inferior race. The fact that Sargon says that when he was a gardener Isthar loved him, might well refer to the cessation of Eve's love for Cain after his murder of Abel.

Apparently taking the legend as true history Professor Sayce comments upon it :

> " The Euphrates refused to drown its future lord,

and bore the child in safety to Akki 'the irrigator,' the representative of the Accadian peasants[1] who tilled the land for their Semitic masters. In this lowly condition and among a subjugated race Sargon was brought up. Akki took compassion on the little waif, and reared him as if he had been his own son. As he grew older he was set to till the garden and to cultivate the fruit trees, and while engaged in this humble work attracted the love of the goddess Istar. Then came the hour of his deliverance from servile employment, and, like David, he made his way to a throne. For long years he ruled the black-headed race." (*Hibbert Lectures*, p. 27.)

The choice lies therefore between this charming and intimate story and my different explanation of the legend, namely, that it is a parody upon the true history of Cain who, adopting the Devil as his adviser, ruled over the pre-Adamites once feared by him.

As an example of the priests' contradictions, Sargon says in this legend that he " knew not his father," while he elsewhere claims Dati-Enlil as his father. Professor King who, like Professor Sayce, takes the inscriptions seriously, says :

"that Shar-Gani-sharri (Sargon) was the actual founder of his dynasty is clear from the inscription upon his gate-sockets found at Nippur, which ascribe no title to his father, Dati-Enlil, proving that his family had not even held the patesiate or governorship of Akkad under the suzerainty of Kish." (*Sumer and Akkad*, p. 232.)

One wonders how authorities who accept these legends as history account for Sargon's contradictory statements as to his origin.

In connection with the different titles given to the Devil, another possibility is suggested here for what it is worth—may not the name Akkad, sometimes applied to Babylonia in inscriptions, have been taken from Akki the Devil, for parts

[1] Note that these " Accadian peasants " were the people (otherwise called Sumerians) whom Assyriologists have brought themselves to accept as the founders of Babylonian civilisation and culture.

of Babylonia seem to have been called after Cain ? The *Cambridge History* speaks of " the Old Khana on the middle Euphrates,"[1] and although Professor Waddell suggests that the name meant the Land of Canes (or reeds) and was descriptive of the original wild aspect of Babylonia,[2] it seems to me as probable that it meant the Land of Cain.   Especially as George Smith writes of a town in Babylonia, called Kan-nan, of which the inhabitants were called Kanunai.   He remarks that they must not be confused with the Canaanites of Phœnicia,[2] but for reasons given in Appendix C., pp. 2, 3, my own belief is that in both cases the names were derived from Cain.

[1] Vol. I, p. 467.   And see above, p. 15.
[2] *Asiatic Review*, April, 1926.
[3] *Chaldean Genesis*, 1880, p. 316.

XXVI

"THE MYSTERY OF INIQUITY"

JUDGING from the frequent mention of a supreme spirit of evil in the Babylonian inscriptions the Devil was more real to the ancient Babylonians than to some modern thinkers. He was, as we have seen, Sargon's rescuer and protector, the donor of Sargon's dominions and subjects, the deity worshipped by Sargon who is called his priest,[1] and he is addressed as the equal or superior of Anu ("the father of the gods" and "king of heaven") in many of the hymns, prayers and incantations. Sheer dread of him must, one would think, have inspired such intercessions as :

> "O divine Enlil father of Sumer, O shepherd of the dark-headed people, O hero who sees by thy own power. Strong lord, directing mankind." (*Religions of Babylonia and Assyria*, M. Jastrow, p. 72.)[2]

Very different sentiments are expressed by such fragments as the following :

" The evil Spirit hath lain in wait in the desert,
Unto the side of the man hath drawn nigh.
The evil genius for ever is rampant
And none can resist him.
The evil Ghost goeth furtively in the desert and
Causeth slaughter among men,
The evil Devil prowleth in the City
It hath no rest (?) from slaughtering men."
(The Devils and Evil Spirits of Babylonia,
R. C. Thompson, Vol. 2, p. 105.)

And there is a grim appropriateness in the title given to Bel in some inscriptions, i.e. " Sin the Uplifter of Horns,"[3]

---

[1] See *ante*, p. 54.
[2] See Appendix F.
[3] See p. 55.

Only a more intimate acquaintance with the evil spirit than we can easily imagine can explain the existence in Babylonia of the great work in seventy-two books (as Professor Sayce describes it) which formed part of Sargon's library, and is called " Observations " or "Illuminations" of Bel.[1] Professor Sayce writes :

> " Up to the time of Berossos, however, it was remembered that the god Bel himself was its traditional author, and the work is sometimes quoted as simply ' Bel '." (*Hibbert Lectures*, p. 29.)
>
> " In the ' Observations of Bel ' the stars are already invested with a divine character. The planets are gods like the sun and moon, and the stars have already been identified with certain deities of the official pantheon, or else have been dedicated to them. The whole heaven, as well as the periods of the moon, has been divided between the three supreme divinities, Anu, Bel and Ea. In fact, there is an astro-theology, a system of sabaism, as it would have been called half a century ago. This astro-theology must go back to the very earliest times. The cuneiform characters alone are a proof of this."
> (p. 400.)

These remarks offer food for reflection. Who, if not the Devil, "the prince of the power of the air," " the spirit that now worketh in the children of disobedience " could have invented this astro-theology, the worship of the whole host of heaven ? That it was invented by an inferior race (probably negroid) is in my opinion out of the question, although some Assyriologists are ready to ascribe it to the " Sumerians."

The Professor writes about the " Observations of Bel " :

> " It was translated in later days into Greek by the historian Berossos ; and though supplemented by

[1] In the Observations of Bel we may trace the origin of human sacrifice, against which practice the Israelites were warned after they left Egypt, where it was carried on by the pagan priests. (Lev. xviii, 21.) Professor Sayce writes :
" In the great work on astronomy called *The Observations of Bel* we are told that ' on the high places the son is burnt ' " (*Hibbert Lectures*, 1887, p. 59), and he remarks that this " proves that the sacrifice of children was a Babylonian institution."

numerous editions in its passage through the hands of generations of Babylonian astronomers, the original work contained so many records of eclipses as to demonstrate the antiquity of Babylonian astronomy even in the remote age of Sargon himself." (*Hibbert Lectures*, p. 29.)

With all due deference I would suggest that those numerous records of eclipses may have been interpolated by later generations of priests. Considering the well-known tendency of ancient historians to exaggerate the antiquity of their nations, such interpolations may have been meant to give the impression that their history went back for thousands of years. If the Devil was the originator of that system of astro-theology it might, of course, have existed for countless ages before Adam, except for the fact that in the " Observations of Bel " the heavens are divided between Anu, Ea and Bel, which suggests that it was invented after the creation of our first parents.

There are other indications that the Devil played a real and substantial part in ancient Babylonia ; he seems, for instance, to have been looked upon as its king-maker. Professor Sayce, describing the inauguration ceremony of the Babylonian kings, writes :

" The claimant to the sovereignty took the hand of Bel, as it was called, and then became the adopted son of the god. Until this ceremony, however much he might be a king de facto he was not so de jure . . . the legal title could be given by Bel and by Bel only." (*Babylonian and Assyrian Life*, p. 36.)

Is it extravagant to suggest that this ceremony may have commemorated an unholy compact between Cain and the Devil —the exiled man and the disgraced spirit ? A Jewish tradition describes how Satan put the thought of murder into Cain's mind ; may we not conclude that in the same way Cain was inspired to establish idolatry ? The drawing given here was thought by George Smith to represent " Bel encountering the Dragon,"[1] but my impression is that in it we see Cain, i.e. Sargon, " taking the hand of Bel." (See illustration facing p. 60.)

[1] *Chaldean Genesis*, p. 95.

Neither in Hebrew nor Babylonian literature are Bel and the Dragon represented as antagonists. They are obviously, on the contrary, different forms of the same god and there is no authority, therefore, for concluding that this drawing represents a fight between the two. It is even possible that the word Dragon came from Dagon which, according to Professor Jastrow, was only another name for Bel.[1] The drawing may, of course, represent the fight between the Sun-god Marduk and Tiamat (a favourite subject with Babylonian artists), in which case we may still see in it a portrait of Cain, under the mythological guise of Marduk or Merodach. (See illustration facing.)

The Bible teaching about the Devil is clear and decisive ; he is mentioned at least fifty times in the New Testament, and yet there is now a marked reluctance to believe in his existence even among the clergy, one of whom writes in the *Encyclopædia Britannica* :

> " The teaching of Jesus even in this matter may be accounted for as either an accommodation to the views of those with whom he was dealing, or more probably as a proof of the limitation of knowledge which was a necessary condition of the Incarnation."
> (Ed. XI, *The Devil*.)

The unwarranted assurance of the last lines needs no comment, but it may well be asked how any modern teacher would like to be accused of accommodating his views to those of his pupils ?

---

[1] M. Jastrow, *Babylonian and Assyrian Religions*, p. 154. And Professor Sayce says : " In W.A.I. (Western Asiatic Inscriptions) III, 68, 21, Dagon is identified with Mul-lil." (*Hibbert Lectures*, 1887, p. 1888.)

THE SUN GOD, MERODACH OR MARDUK   [See pp. 79–100.

Reproduced by permission from "Chaldean Genesis," by G. Smith, published by Messrs. Sampson
Low, Marston and Co. Ltd.

[Face p. 100

XXVII

THE CHILDREN OF BEL

STARTLING possibilities are suggested by the fact that Sargon is said to have reigned over the " children of Bel "[1] and the " realm of Enlil,"[2] and that his subjects the " blackheads " were entrusted to him by Akki (another name for the Devil). A problem faces us which we cannot hope to solve—why were these people thus stigmatised as belonging to the Devil ? All that is plain to us is that, according to the Bible and the Babylonian inscriptions two non-Adamite races existed in the beginning of history. The people who Cain feared might kill him, and among whom he finally built a city were evidently the " blackheads " over whom Sargon ruled, and who must have existed before Adam, while the other race of evil fame which trod the earth in Cain's lifetime is shown by both the Bible and Babylonian monuments to have been half human— half spirit. These people are called in the Bible the Nephilim, Rephaim, or Fallen Ones, and are said to have been the children of fallen angels who took as wives the daughters of men.

As Professor King points out, a parallel is provided in the Babylonian inscriptions :

> " to the circumstances preceding the birth of the Nephilim at the beginning of the sixth chapter of Genesis, for in them also great prowess or distinction is ascribed to the progeny of human and divine unions. According to the traditions the records embody, the Sumerians looked back to a time when gods lived upon the earth with men . . . we read of two Sumerian heroes, also rulers of cities who were divine on the father's or mother's side but not on both." (*Legends of Babylon and Egypt*, p. 39.)

[1] *The First Bible*. Conder. See *ante* p. 54.
[2] *Sumer and Akkad*. L. King, p. 242.

The inscriptions describe this pre-historic race as half-man and half-animal. From the Cutha Tablet of Creation come the words:

"Men with the bodies of birds of the desert, human beings with the faces of ravens, these the great gods created, and in the earth the gods created for them a dwelling. Tiamat gave unto them strength, their life the mistress of the gods raised. . . . In the first days the evil gods, the angels who were in rebellion, who in the lower part of heaven had been created, they caused their evil work devising with wicked heads ruling to the river. There were seven of them. The first was . . . the second was a great animal . . . the third was a leopard . . . the fourth was a serpent . . . the fifth was a terrible . . . the sixth was a striker which to god and king did not submit, the seventh was the messenger of the evil wind, etc." (*Chaldean Genesis*, pp. 103-107.)

Rigmarole though all this is, one feels that in it grim truths are hinted at, and that the Babylonian scribes knew more about that hybrid race than we learn from the Bible. In Deut. iii, 11, where Og, the king of Bashan, is said to be " of the remnant of the giants," the Hebrew word translated giants is " rapha " or " raphaim,"[1] and really means a sort of monster, a " fearful one," not a gigantic man like Nimrod, who is described in Hebrew as a " gibbor," which means giant. This may explain the fact that the Israelites who seem to have easily exterminated those people in the end, were terrified of them at first.

The existence of these races, witnessed to by both the Bible and the Babylonian writings, is apparently ignored by scientists. Yet may it not account for the perplexing bones found from time to time in different parts of the world? May we not ascribe to those races the Pithecanthropus Erectus, the Man of Heidelberg, the Neanderthal Man, the Negroid of Grimaldi, the Galley Hill Man, the Lemur-monkey Man, etc.—the fearsome ancestors with whom some anthropologists have been ready to saddle themselves and us? It is reassuring to think that the gorilla-like " Taung's skull," claimed as the missing link

[1] Or " Nephilim." See p. 105.

A " SUMERIAN "   [See p. 102.

Reproduced from King's " A History of Sumer and Akkad," by permission of
the Publishers, Messrs. Chatto and Windus.

[Photo : W. F. Mansell.

[Face p. 102.

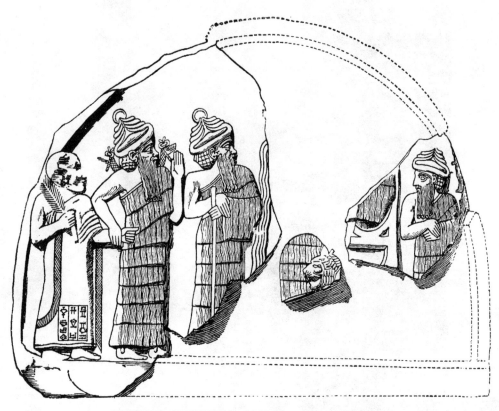

THREE SEMITES AND A "SUMERIAN"

See p. 103.

Reproduced from King's "A History of Sumer and Akkad," by permission of the Publishers, Messrs. Chatto and Windus.

[Face p. 103.

between man and the ape family by Professor Haeckel, need have had no connection with Adam's race since it may be a relic of that half-human race.

While Professor Sayce thinks that the people called " Children of Bel " and " the black-heads " in inscriptions were probably negroid,[1] other authorities, on the strength of certain drawings upon the monuments, believe them to have been of a very peculiar type, white people perhaps, but certainly abnormal. These peculiar people are supposed to have been the Sumerians, who, according to the Sumerian school, invented the art of writing.

The above was described in an illustrated paper as " the men whose supreme gift to Babylonia was the art of writing." (*The Sphere*, October 11th, 1924.) (See facing page 102.)

To my mind, drawings like the above are the product of the priests' frivolity, malignity or inanity, and in keeping with the " mongrel dialect " of the inscriptions and the contradictory character and mocking tone of their contents. According to Professor King, the earliest Babylonian monuments show both this degraded type of man which he calls Sumerian and a superior type which he calls Semitic. The former are, to my mind, mere caricatures of human beings, but the latter, in spite of the mock archaic style of the work, are evidently Adamites and are distinctly like Europeans.

Professor King writes :

" Excavations have not contributed to the solution of the problems as to the period at which Sumerians and Semites first came in contact, or which race was first in possession of the land." (*Sumer and Akkad*, p. 40.)

In view of this admission it seems strange that he should have ventured to place a formidable array of Sumerian kings before the so-called Semitic dynasty of Sargon. The fact that according to him some of those kings are credited in inscriptions with the same achievements as Sargon[2] supports my theory that they were entirely fictitious, and that much of the priests' information is false.

[1] See above, p. 15.
[2] See Appendix D.

XXVIII

SUGGESTIVE NAMES IN INSCRIPTIONS

IN the mythological inscriptions we find two kinds of spirits who, I believe, represent respectively Cain's race and the pre-Adamites. Since the name Annunaki undoubtedly connects one kind of spirits with Anu (Adam), who is called the king of the Annunaki, the other name Igigi presumably stands for the pre-Adamites. Professor Jastrow says that the priests appealed to the Annunaki as gods, and quotes the inscription :

> " He who fears the Annunaki will lengthen his days." (*Religion of Egypt and Assyria*, p. 389.)

Although, as usual, the priests obscured the truth by sometimes representing the Annunaki as the " evil spirits of the deep," as opposed to the " Igigi or spirits of heaven," it seems certain that the Annunaki were the white race and the Igigi the black. The priests perhaps are nearer the truth when they say that the gods :

> " manifest their anger against the Igigi. They are sent out by them to do service and are shown to be severe and cruel ; not favourable to man but hostile to him." (*Religion of Egypt and Assyria*, p. 307.)

The gods, as Professor Meyer points out,[1] are always represented on the monuments as " Semites " (Adamites), so it is clear that the Annunaki who are appealed to as gods were the white race ; and as the inscription given below says that Marduk, whom I regard as Cain's mythological representative, was " great among the Igigi," I presume that they were the black-heads or negroes[2] over whom Cain ruled.

[1] Quoted by Professor King. *Sumer and Akkad*, p. 49.
[2] Merodach is called Asari, " Nourisher of the black-headed race." (*Hibbert Lectures*, p. 287.)

The inscription runs :

" When the supreme Anu king of the Annunaki, and Enlil, the Lord of Heaven and Earth, who fixes the destiny of the land, had committed to Marduk the first born of the earth [Ea] the rule of all mankind, making him great among the Igigi, etc." (M. Jastrow, *Religion in Babylonia and Assyria*, p. 35.)

There is, of course, the possibility that the Igigi were the half-human race, but on the whole it seems more likely that they were the black-heads mentioned in Sargon's inscriptions, and the Nigilma of the following " Sumerian " account of the Creation.[1]

Professor King gives the translation and, of course, adds the punctuation, the accuracy of which I take the liberty of questioning :

" When Anu, Enlil Enki and Ninkharsagga
Created the blackheaded (i.e. mankind),
The niggil (ma) of the earth they caused the earth
    to produce (?),
The animals, the four-legged creatures of the field,
    they artfully called into existence."
                (*Legends of Babylon and Egypt*, p. 56.)

My reading of the above passage would be—" When Anu, Enlil, Enki and Ninkharsagga created the black-headed the niggilma of the earth, they caused the earth to produce the animals, the four-legged creatures of the field they artfully called into existence," according to which " the black-headed " and " the niggilma " mean the same thing, and represent, in my opinion, the pre-Adamites. We may reasonably conjecture that the word Igigi, especially if identified with the black-headed Niggilma, may contain the root of the word Niger (black), Negro or Nigger.

---

[1] George Smith says Sargon ruled the people of " the black-face." (*Chaldean Genesis*, p. 82.)

H

XXIX

CAIN UNDER ANOTHER NAME

THE following legend is, to my mind, a link between Babylonia and ancient Rome, and a clue to the problem of the priest-kings of Nemi, the theme of Sir James Frazer's work *The Golden Bough*. This story forms part of the *Legends of Izdubar* (otherwise called Gilgames), which are thought to have been written about the time of Hammurabi (2000 B.C.).[1] In this story Abel is referred to, according to Professor Sayce, under two different names—Tammuz and Taballu; Eve, in my opinion, is represented by Isthar, and Cain by the gardener Isullanu, of whom Professor Sayce writes:

> "Isullanu the gardener of Anu is probably the mystic prototype of the historical Sargon of Akkad whom later legend turned into a gardener beloved by the goddess Istar." (*Hibbert Legends*, p. 250.)

It is strange that Professor Sayce connects Isullanu with Sargon and not with Cain, especially as the probability of Cain's presence in Babylonia is admitted by him, for the fact that the shepherd Taballu is, according to him, the double of Abel and that Istar is, as we have seen, the mythological form of Eve, seems to make that connection so evident. The fact, too, that Isullanu calls Isthar "Mother," and is said to be the gardener of Isthar's father (as Anu, otherwise Adam, is sometimes called in the inscriptions) is additional proof that Isullanu represents Cain. It is also suggestive that, as the Professor tells us, the name Isullanu meant "he who makes green the living things," which harmonises with the description of Cain in the Bible—a tiller of the ground. That the Professor identifies Isullanu with Sargon, however, suits my purpose even better, since it offers another reason for identifying Sargon with Cain.

[1] *Chaldean Genesis*, p. 168.

In this curious legend (a good example of the priests' nonsense) the goddess Isthar is taunted by the hero Izdubar with ficklencss and cruelty, and that this libels our first mother's character may be gathered from the excellent qualities attributed to her at other times, and also when she is represented as the god Ea, who is described as a benevolent deity, teaching the art of healing and culture to mankind.[1] Professor Sayce notices the contradictory character given to Isthar.

He writes :

> " But who was the goddess whom one legend made the faithful wife enduring even death for her husband's sake, while another regarded her as the most faithless and cruel of coquettes ? " (*Hibbert Lectures*, p. 250.)

The Legend runs :

" 1. For the favour of Gisdhubar the princess Isthar lifted the eyes ;
2. (Look up), Gisdhubar, and be thou my bridegroom!
3. I am thy vine, thou art its bond ;
4. Be thou my husband and I will be thy wife.
5. I will give thee a chariot of crystal and gold, [etc.]
17. (Gisdhubar) opened his mouth and speaks,
18. (he says thus) to the princess Istar :
19. (I will leave) to thyself thy possession,
20. (in thy realm are) corpses and corruption (?)
21. . . . disease and famine.
30. The palace is the destroyer of heroes
31. A deceitful (?) mouth are its hidden recesses
37. Never may I be (thy) bridegroom for ever.
38. Never may a god make thee joyous.
41. To Tammuz the bridegroom (of thy youth) thou didst look ;
42. year after year with weeping didst thou cling to him.
43. Alala, the eagle, also didst thou love ;

---

[1] Ea is said to be merciful, compassionate, wise, sentient and pure. (*Hibbert Lectures*, 1887, pp. 140-141.) Also " the author of knowledge and intelligence." (Ditto, p. 118.)

44. Thou didst strike him and break his wings ;
45. he remained in the forest ; he begged for his wings.
46. Thou didst love, too, a lion perfect in might ;
47. seven by seven didst thou tear out his teeth, seven by seven.
48. And thou didst love a horse glorious in battle ;
53. Thou didst love also the shepherd Taballu,
54. who continually poured out for thee the smoke (of sacrifice)
56. thou didst bring him forth and into a hyena didst change him ;
58. and his own dogs tore his wounds.
59. Moreover, thou didst love Isullanu the gardener of thy father,
60. who was ever raising for thee costly trees.
61. Every day had he made bright thy dish.
62. Thou didst take from him (his eye) and didst mock him :
63. O my Isullanu, come, let us eat thine abundant store,
64. and bring out thy hand and dismiss all fear of us.
65. Isullanu says to thee :
66. As for me, what dost thou ask of me ?
67. O my mother, thou cookest not (and) I eat not ;
68. the food I have eaten are garlands and girdles ;
69. the prison of the hurricane is (thy) hidden recess.
70. Thou didst listen and (didst impose) punishment ;
71. thou didst strike him ; to bondage thou didst (assign him) ;
72. and thou madest him sit in the midst of (a tomb ?)."

(*Hibbert Lectures*, p. 246.)

My proposition that in this Babylonian legend there lies a clue to the problem of the Grove of Nemi can hardly be regarded as far-fetched, considering that the Greek and Roman mythologies were derived from the Babylonians.[1]

We have seen that Professor Sayce regards the gardener Isullanu as representing Sargon, which justifies us in regarding

[1] " The Greeks, borrowing most of their astronomical knowledge from the Babylonians, held similar myths and ideas. . . . The Romans adopted the Greek ideas." (*Ency. Brit.*, Ed. II, Canis Major.)

him as Cain ; we have also seen that the Professor identifies Tammuz with Abel, and the fact that in the above legend he regards Tammuz and Taballu as one and the same[1] justifies us in looking for a double character in the Roman legend as well. This we find in the goddess Diana (admittedly a form of Isthar[2]) and the water-nymph Egeria who is shown by her attributes to be another form of Isthar. That both these characters represent Eve seems obvious, for Verbius, the young hero of the Grove is connected by Sir James Frazer with Tammuz and therefore with Abel. Having satisfied ourselves therefore that Cain's mother and brother are represented in both the Babylonian and Roman legends, it seems natural to look for Cain himself ; and since Professor Sayce identifies the gardener Isullanu in the Babylonian legend with Sargon it seems evident that the murderer priest king of the Roman legend represents Cain.

This possibility increases the interest of the legend, about which Sir James Frazer writes :

> " Who does not know Turner's picture of the Golden Bough ? The little woodland lake of Nemi— ' Diana's Mirror ' as it was called by the ancients, that calm water lapped in a green hollow of the Alban Hills . . . in antiquity this sylvan landscape was the scene of a strange and recurring tragedy . . . dark crimes were perpetrated there under the mask of religion."

The same writer quotes Macaulay's verse :

> " The still glassy lake that sleeps
> Beneath Aricia's trees—
> These trees in whose dim shadow
> The ghastly priest doth reign
> The priest who slew the slayer
> And shall himself be slain."

Why, Sir James Frazer asks, had the priest of Nemi to slay his predecessor ? And why, before doing so, had he to pluck the branch of a certain tree which the public opinion of the

[1] See p. 82.
[2] See Appendix FA.

ancients identified with the Golden Bough? The answer I venture to give is : Because Cain murdered Abel, whose sacrificial offering had been preferred to his own, and because the sacred tree, round which the priest prowled incessantly, commemorated the tree of the Garden of Eden which had so largely influenced the destiny of Adam's family.

To anyone who accepts my arguments and is willing to regard the priest-king of Nemi as derived from Cain, the following account of a double-headed bust[1] found at Nemi and believed to represent the priest-king will be of interest. Sir James Frazer suggests that the older head may represent the actual priest-king and the younger head the murderer who was to kill him and take his place. My own suggestion is that the older head represents Cain—the murderer priest-king—while in the younger head I see his brother Abel. Sir James Frazer, describing the bust says :

> "The type of face is similar in both heads but there are marked differences between them—for while the one is young and beardless with shut lips and a steadfast gaze, the other is a man of middle life with a long and matted beard, wrinkled brows, a wild and anxious look in his eyes and an open grinning mouth, but perhaps the most singular thing about the two heads is the leaves with scalloped edges which are plastered, so to say, on the necks of both busts and apparently also under the eyes of the younger figure. The leaves have been interpreted as oak leaves and the moustache of the older figure clearly resembles an oakleaf. All this may contain in germ the solution of the problem of the king of the wood worship."
> (*The Golden Bough.*)

The likeness between the two faces of the bust supports my theory that they represent the brothers Cain and Abel, while the difference of age and expression accords with the story told about them in Genesis ; and more support for my theory may perhaps be found in the "open grinning mouth" of the older face, which is clearly one-sided and, therefore, suggestive of a muscular contortion known to science as "the Cynic spasm,"

[1] See Frontispiece.

and described as " a convulsive spasm of the muscles of one side of the face, distorting the mouth, nose, etc. into the appearance of a grin."[1]

To one who has decided upon grounds already stated that the face of the murderer-king in the Roman bust represents Cain it naturally seems more than a coincidence that the muscular contortion, with which he is portrayed, has been given a name containing the root of the word Cain and apparently associated in other ways as well with Cain.

Philologists agree that the word " Cynics " (Kynikoi) given to certain Greek philosophers in the first century A.D. came from the Greek word for dog (Kuon) and that those philosophers were so-called because they were " prone to fall back into animalism pure and simple,"[2] and are said to " have outraged the dictates of common decency,"[3] but the idea that the Greek word for dog may have been derived from the name of Cain is entirely my own and since I cannot claim to be one of Cowper's

> " learned philologists who chase
> A panting syllable through time and space,"

my reasons for so bold a suggestion must be stated.

Philologically speaking it is a reasonable suggestion, for the word kuon (dog) is quite as like the word Cain as is the second syllable of Sargon's name which is identified with " Cain " ;[4] and historically speaking a connection between the words Cain, Cynic and dog seems probable for, while the Epistle of Jude indicates that the evil character of Cain's later life was known to the Apostles, St. Paul and St. John head their lists of evil-doers with the word " dogs," which one modern translator of the Bible has changed into " Cynics,"[5] a more convincing rendering than " dogs," for obviously men and not animals are referred to.

Cain's wickedness, which was thus vividly remembered in Palestine in the Apostles' time, can scarcely have been lost

[1] *Century Dictionary* (Cynic spasm).
[2] *Ency. Brit.* Ed. II, Cynics.
[3] Ditto.
[4] See p. 31.
[5] Ferrar Fenton, *Bible in Modern English.*

sight of in ancient Babylonia if he was Sargon of Akkad, although, perhaps, his great achievements overshadowed it and the priests may have concealed it in their Mysteries. The truth however was flimsily disguised in Babylonia, and it seems possible that Sargon's true character was sufficiently recognised there to have caused his name to be given to dogs which were abominated in the ancient East :

> " In the Old and New Testaments the dog is spoken of almost with abhorrence ; it ranked amongst the unclean beasts ; traffic in it was considered as an abomination." (*Ency. Brit.*, Ed. XI, Dogs.)

The Cynics of Greece were evidently proud of their opprobrious title for they adopted a dog as their emblem or badge.[1] Perhaps they knew that dogs originally took the name Kuon from Cain, and gloried in the fact, for in the second century A.D. another sect of philosophers arose who announced their preference for Cain over Abel, and were called Cainites :

> " They believed that Cain derived his existence from the superior power and Abel from the inferior power." (*Ency. Brit.*, Ed. XI, Cain.)

Although to some minds the idea may seem fantastic, these considerations suffice to convince me that a connection exists between the names Cain and Sargon, Kuon, the Greek word for dog, and the kyni-koi or Cynics of Greece ; and that through the sculptured grin and the " Cynic spasm," the " King of the Wood " may be identified with Cain.

Was Canis the Dog-star called after Cain ? Homer wrote of it

> " Whose breath
> Taints the red air with fevers, plagues, and death."[2]

---

[1] " It is noticeable that the Cynics agreed in taking a dog as their common badge or symbol." (*Ency. Brit.*, Ed. XI, Cynics.)

[2] It was included in the Babylonian stellar system. (*Ency. Brit.*, Ed. Canis.) Merodach, whom we have identified with Cain, is represented as accompanied by four dogs, Uccumu " the despoiler," Acculu " the devourer," Icsuda " the capturer," and Iltebu the " carrier-away." (*The Chaldean Genesis*, 1880, p. 190.)

PART TWO

I

IN THE GREY DAWN OF HISTORY

HAPPILY Cain's followers, like most conspirators, bungled badly and let the truth come down to us through their elaborate barrier of lies. The overwhelming proof that the Babylonians knew of God's existence and wilfully disguised that fact is in our possession.

Although, as we have seen, the mythological writings constantly allude to the personages mentioned in the first chapters of Genesis, no allusion is made in them to the Creator, the knowledge of Whom has come down to us through the Hebrew race.

According to the Babylonian priests, several gods took part in the creation of the world, and the gods Anu, Ea and Bel at first, and in later times Shamas, Istar and Sin ruled the heavens, earth, sea and " the affairs of men." No room is left in the Babylonian pantheon for a Supreme Being. Three or four tablets have been found, however, smothered as it were among thousands of polytheistic inscriptions, which clearly show that the knowledge of God existed in Babylonia before the year 2200 B.C., when there is said to have been a " literary revival " during which older writings and traditions were reproduced. These monotheistic writings may, therefore, have existed in Sargon's time, and may have owed their origin to him.

In spite of the fact that many generations of priests have handled these inscriptions, their style is clear and lucid in comparison with all the mythological writings ; and this is another proof that the archaic character of the latter was affected. These inscriptions telling about One Supreme Being, the rebellious angels and the Fall of Adam, and which are known to be among the oldest Babylonian writings, prove the soundness of Dr. Kittel's theory that a common source existed for the Bible and the Babylonian inscriptions, and that that source was a monotheistic one ; to use his words " very ancient knowledge imparted by God to man."

Other scholars have held the opinion that the original source of both the Bible and Babylonian writings was polytheistic, and credit the Israelitish prophets with the change to monotheism.

They ignore the possibility that instead of the Hebrews transforming the polytheistic religion of the Babylonians, the Babylonians may have corrupted an original monotheistic religion preserved by the Hebrews. Surely, considering the tendency of the human race to adopt paganism, it is more reasonable to conclude that One God was exchanged for many gods than that many gods were merged into One.

Professor Delitzsch concluded that the monotheistic religion belonged to Sargon's race (according to him the North Semitic race) and that the polytheistic religion belonged to the inferior race of Babylonia. He writes :

> " These North Semitic tribes . . . thought of and worshipped God as a single spiritual being, and were in possession of religious ideas which differed from the indigenous polytheistic mode of thought in Babylonia." (*Laws of Moses. The Code of Hammurabi*, p. 27, S. A. Cooke.)

Professor Sayce, on the contrary, has concluded that the monotheistic religion belonged to the " Sumerians." He says :

> " In the pre-Semitic days of Chaldea a monotheistic school had flourished. . . . But this school died out."

and suggests that the polytheistic religion was imported by the so-called Semitic race.

> " The theology of Babylonia as it is known to us is thus an artificial product. It combines two wholly different forms of faith and religious conception. One of these was overlaid by the other at a very early period in the history of the people . . . and the theological beliefs of Sumer received a Semitic interpretation." (*Religions of Egypt and Babylonia.*)

The Professor, in an evident attempt to account for the sure signs that the conception of a Supreme God once existed in Babylonia, although He was not worshipped there, conjectures as follows :

> "The higher minds of the nation struggled now and again towards the conception of One Supreme God and of a purer form of faith, but the dead weight of polytheistic beliefs and practices prevented them from ever really reaching it." (*Assyria, its Princes, etc.*, p. 85.)

Although these authorities differ as to which race possessed the knowledge of One God and as to which form of religion was the earlier in Babylonia, their admissions that that knowledge existed there side by side with the worship of other gods support my claim that Cain introduced that knowledge, and used it as the basis of idolatry by ascribing Divine attributes to the gods of his own invention.

II

CAIN'S PENITENTIAL HYMN

ONE of the monotheistic inscriptions is called " the penitential hymn," and the words of it are such as might have been uttered by Cain himself. Professor Sayce translates it thus :

> " The transgression I have committed I knew not. The sin that I sinned I knew not. The forbidden thing did I trample on. My Lord in the wrath of his heart has overpowered me. God who knew (though I knew not) hath pierced me. . . . I lay on the ground and no man seized me by the hand. I wept and my palms none took. I cried aloud and there was none that could hear me. I am in darkness and trouble. I lifted not myself up. To my God I referred my (distress). My prayer I addressed . . . How long O my God shall I suffer ? How long O my God who knewest (though) I knew not shall thy heart be wrath ? " (*Schweich Lectures*, 1908, p. 23.)

This prayer was discovered in the ruins of Assur-bani-pal's palace ; the priests of that king's reign (seventh century B.C.) had presumably copied it from older tablets. Professor King tells us that " a detailed study of these inscriptions proves " that all the writings in the ruins of that palace were copies of more ancient ones.

At the time the " penitential hymn " was finally copied the gods of Babylonia were legion. According to an inscription of King Assur-bani-pal, there were 6,500 of them in his land, yet the words of this prayer are those of a believer in One God. Do they express Cain's agony of mind before, under the Devil's influence, he hardened his heart and invented his plan of revenge ? In the reiterated words " who knew though I knew not " we may find a sign of the coming resentment and rebellion.

Many " penitential hymns " have been discovered but, so far as I know, this is the only copy free from paganism. Professor Sayce gives what is obviously another version of the hymn in which these lines occur :

> " May God be appeased again, for I knew not that I
>   sinned.
> May Istar, my mother, be appeased again, for I knew
>   not that I sinned,
> God knoweth that I knew not : may he be appeased.
> Istar, my mother, knoweth that I knew not : may
>   she be appeased.
> May the heart of my God be appeased.
> May God and Istar, my mother, be appeased. [etc.] . . .
> God, in the strength of his heart, has taken me.
> Istar, my mother, has seized upon me, and put me
>   to grief, [etc.]."

The priests' fashion of mythologising is well exemplified by this (probably later) version of the " penitential hymn." The fact that the penitent calls Isthar (Eve) " mother," and was evidently under her displeasure, supports my theory that the hymn was originally inspired by words which Cain had once uttered, or might have been supposed to have uttered. Commenting upon this version of the hymn, Professor Sayce writes :

> " A rubric is attached to this verse, stating that it is to be repeated ten times, and at the end of the whole psalm is the further rubric : ' For the tearful supplication of the heart let the glorious name of every god be invoked sixty-five times, and then the heart shall have peace '." (*Assyria : its Princes, Priests, etc.*, p. 73.)[1]

A second monotheistic inscription undoubtedly refers to the fall of the rebellious angels to whose existence both the Old and New Testaments witness.

The translator says :

> " The first four lines are broken. They related, no doubt, that a festival of praise and thanksgiving was being held in heaven, when this rebellion took place."

[1] The rubric is evidently later priests' directions.

The inscription runs :

> " The Divine Being spoke three times, the com-
> mencement of a psalm.
> 6. The god of holy songs, Lord of religion and
>   worship
> 7. seated a thousand singers and musicians: and
>   established a choral band
> 8. who to his hymn were to respond in multitudes . . .
> 9. With a loud cry of contempt they broke up his
>   holy song
> 10. spoiling, confusing, confounding, his hymn of
>   praise.
> 11. The god of a bright crown with a wish to summon
>   his adherents
> 12. sounded a trumpet blast which would wake the
>   dead,
> 13. Which to those rebel angels prohibited return,
> 14. he stopped their service, and sent them to the
>   gods who were his enemies
> 15. In their room he created mankind.
> 16. The first who received life, dwelt along with him.
> 17. May he give them strength, never to neglect his
>   word,
> 18. Following the serpent's voice, whom his hands had
>   made."
>
> (*Records of the Past*, Vol. 7, p. 127.)

The translator remarks that the mediæval church also held
the opinion that mankind was created to fill up the void in
creation caused by the rebellion of the ungrateful angels.
With regard to the different titles given to the Supreme Being,
the translator says that the Assyrian scribe :

> " annotates in the margin that the same god is meant
> throughout, under all these different epithets."

One wonders what more the priestly scribe could have
explained if he had chosen. That he knew all that we learn
from the first chapters of Genesis can scarcely be doubted.

Another monotheistic inscription is called by its translator

TRIAL OF ADAM   [See p. 121.

Reproduced by permission from " Phoenician Origin of Britons, Scots and Anglo-Saxons," by Prof. L. A. Waddell.   Published by Messrs. Williams and Norgate.

BABYLONIAN CYLINDER SEAL   [See p. 138.

Reproduced from King's " A History of Sumer and Akkad," by permission of the Publishers, Messrs. Chatto and Windus.

[Face p. 121

(Professor Chiera of Pennsylvania) " God's words to Adam."[1] The Professor points out that God's speech apparently ends in the blessing on man, which supports his interpretation of the story that Adam was driven from Eden to prevent him obtaining food which might make him immortal. The inscription runs :

> " Thy humanity, thy body has not been freed. For mankind words of wisdom are not. Finish thy weeping. From my presence go to the desert. As an outcast thou shalt not return to my field for working it. As an outcast thou shalt not return to my land for working it. . . . As an hunted one thou shalt not return. Go, work the land, raise food for eating. Humanity thou shalt know abundance." (*Daily Express*, October 26th, 1922, the New York Correspondent.)

This inscription is attributed by the Professor to about the year 2100 B.C. It was found in the ruins of the temple at Nippur, where the University of the Pennsylvania Expedition has excavated several thousands of tablets. The contrast between these dignified words and the Babylonian drawing given below speaks for itself. Professor Waddell from whose work the drawing is reproduced calls it " The Trial of Adam the son of God," and remarks that the " accuser is the Moon-god of Darkness and Death."[2] (See illustration facing.)

The inconsistency of addressing such words as the following to an insignificant local form of the goddess Isthar has impressed Professor Sayce, who says :

> " The old bilingual hymn to the moon-god Nannar of Ur is more suitable for a supreme Baal than for a local moon-god."

The words of this hymn are :

> " Father, long suffering and full of forgiveness, whose hand upholds the life of all mankind, Lord, thy divinity, like the far off heaven, fills the wide

---

[1] The word Adam has been " found used as a proper name in tablets from Tello of the age of Sargon of Akkad." (*Archæology of the Inscriptions*, p. 91, Sayce.)

[2] *Phœnician Origin of the Britons*, pp. 239-253.

sea with fear. . . . First-born, omnipotent, whose heart is immensity and there is none who shall discern it . . . Lord the ordainer of the laws of heaven and earth, whose command may not be (broken) . . . In heaven, who is supreme? Thou alone, thou art supreme! As for thee, thy will is made known on earth, and the spirits below kiss the ground. As for thee, thy will is blown on high like the wind: the stall and the fold are quickened. As for thee, thy will is done on the earth, and the herb grows green." (*Gifford Lectures*, p. 320.)

What explanation can be offered for the existence in a pagan land of words so reminiscent of the Hebrew sacred writings, except that the knowledge of God had once existed there ; and how otherwise can we explain the fact that :

" The conception of a divine messenger or angel who carried the orders of the higher god from heaven to earth and interpreted his will to men, goes back to an early period in the history of Babylonian religion, the Sukkal or angel plays an important part in Babylonian theology." (*Religion of the Babylonians*, Sayce, p. 361.)

Modern churchmen who prefer to ascribe the teaching of " those fundamental beliefs about God and about man on which the Christian religion reposes " to the period of the later prophets,[1] can scarcely be aware of these Babylonian writings which prove that an exalted conception of God had reached Babylonia before 2000 B.C. Surely this is the discovery which Professor Kittel foresaw would refute the attacks made upon the historical truth of the first chapters of Genesis.

[1] *Doctrine of the Infallible Book*, Canon Gore, p. 14.

III

DID CAIN FOUND THE BABYLONIAN LAWS?

THE theory that Cain brought the knowledge of God and of His laws into Babylonia offers, I contend, the best explanation of the resemblance between the laws of Moses and the Babylonian Code called after King Hammurabi (circa 1900 B.C.), who is thought to have been Abraham's contemporary (Amraphæl) ; and this theory is supported by Babylonian inscriptions in which Sargon is called " the deviser of constituted law," " the deviser of prosperity " or " the very wise."[1]

Because of certain resemblances between these Hebrew and Babylonian laws it has been conjectured that the Ten Commandments were based upon the Babylonian Code, of which one writer says :

> " This is the oldest (known) code in the world . . . it is perhaps a thousand years older than Moses, the laws themselves must have been in operation long before their codification and promulgation by Hammurabi. And already the question of the relationship between the Mosaic legislation and that of this great oriental ruler and the possible dependence in parts at least of the former upon the latter, have been much discussed, and have given rise to a considerable literature." (*One Vol. Bible Commentary*, p. 35.)

Curiously enough, while the dependence of the Mosaic law upon the Babylonian is often suggested, the possibility that both may be more or less altered copies of the same original seems to be overlooked, although there is good reason to believe that this was the case.

One writer says :

> " There is not the slightest reason to suppose that

[1] *Hibbert Lectures*, p. 28, Sayce.

Hammurabi introduced a series of innovations or novelties; his laws have had a lengthy history behind them, and prove themselves to be based upon ancient customs. Israelite tradition, in like manner, presupposes laws before Moses, and the two systems of legislation have this in common therefore, that they may claim to be not original productions but authoritative promulgations." (*The Laws of Moses and Hammurabi*, S. A. Cooke, p. 42.)

Since, therefore, " Israelite tradition " is said to " presuppose the existence of laws before Moses,"[1] it may be supposed that certain rules of conduct were laid down in the beginning for Adam and his descendants, and that a solemn reassertion of those Divine rules was made necessary by the falling away of the Israelites during their stay in Egypt. It is also reasonable to suppose that since the Babylonian laws are believed to have been founded upon much older ones, Cain, who would naturally have learnt the rules given to Adam, may have founded those laws upon them.

Another writer says :

" Fragments of law exist which antedate Hammurabi's age, which reveal an organised life not inferior in its cultural developments to that attested by his code. The earlier period has the merit of initiative and attainment, the later adopted and imitated and not infrequently imitated badly . . . we must not forget that previous to Hammurabi there existed a high culture and social developments underestimated." (*Religions of Egypt and Babylonia*, Hugo Winckler.)

This admission that Hammurabi's laws were a bad imitation of older laws, agrees with my theory that the Divine rules given to Adam were to a certain extent the pattern upon which Cain founded his Babylonian laws. The fact that the greatest commandments—those against idolatry and murder are omitted in the Babylonian code while sorcery and witchcraft are encouraged certainly seems to betray his editorship.

[1] See footnote p. 12.

One inscription suggests that Cain gloried in his perversion of the Divine laws and in the part which the Devil had played in that perversion; for, as Sargon, he is made to say that he "had extended his protection over the city of Harran, and according to the ordinance of Anu and Dagon[1] had written down their laws."[2]

The following monotheistic clause in the otherwise poly-theistic code is illuminating; it might almost be thought to belong to the Book of Exodus:

> "If in a sheepfold a stroke of God has taken place, or a lion has killed, the shepherd shall purge himself before God and the accident to the fold the owner of the fold shall face it." (*One Vol. Bible Commentary*, p. 35.)

This obvious reference to God calls for more attention than it has received, considering that Hammurabi's Code begins with what might be called a dedication to the gods Anu, Ea, Bel and Marduk.

Apart from a few more references of the same kind the code is entirely pagan, and deals first with sorcery which was evidently encouraged by the priest lawyers of Babylonia. We read:

> "If a man weave a spell and put a ban upon a man and has not justified himself, he shall be put to death. . . . If a man put a spell upon a man and has not justified himself, he upon whom the spell is laid . . . shall plunge into the holy river, and if the river overcome him he who wove the spell shall take his house. If the holy river makes that man to be innocent and has saved him he who laid the spell upon him shall be put to death." (*One Vol. Bible Commentary*, p. 35.)

Both the resemblances and differences between the Baby-

---

[1] See p. 100. Dagon, another name for Bel the Devil.
[2] *Hibbert Lectures*, p. 188. Merodach, with whom I connect Sargon, is called "the director of the laws of Anu, Bel (Mul-lil) and Ea." (*Hibbert Lectures*, p. 284, 1887.)

lonian and Mosaic laws can be accounted for if we accept the theory that all those laws were founded upon the original rules of conduct given to Adam, that they were taken by Cain into Babylonia and there remodelled to suit his purposes, while on the other hand they were merely reasserted through Moses to the Israelites in the wilderness.

IV

THE LEAVEN OF MALICE AND WICKEDNESS

THAT Cain, the first murderer and idolator, should have suppressed the two greatest commandments is only what we should expect, and we need not hesitate to ascribe to him the worst practices connected with the pagan religions of all times ; for if Cain was, as I have tried to show, the human original of the Babylonian Sun-god whose followers spread a high grade of civilisation all over the ancient world,[1] the nature of the religion which accompanied that civilisation witnesses against him.

Wherever the " Children of the Sun " raised their pyramids and dolmens, their stately palaces and temples, and carried on their irrigation and mining operations, their stone and metal works, they seem to have introduced the grossest superstitions, as well as human sacrifice and cannibalism, all of which, as we have seen, can be traced back to Sargon.[2]

The eating of human flesh was practised in ancient Babylonia[3] and it is reasonable to suppose that Sargon, the great high priest of Enlil (the Devil) should have instituted that custom. Who but Cain, who was " of that evil one," could have invented it ? Next to the worship of false gods what more diabolical insult could be offered to the Almighty than the brutalisation of His noblest creation Man by the eating of human flesh ?

The merciless nature of the Babylonian laws is commented upon by one writer who says :

" The familiar Semitic conceptions of the sacredness
of blood whether human or animal must have long

---

[1] " Wherever it is possible to examine the ruling classes of the archaic civilisation, it is found that they were what are termed gods, that they had the attributes of gods, and that they usually called themselves ' the Children of the Sun '." (*Children of the Sun*, p. 141, W. J. Perry.)

[2] See p. 58, and see Appendices E and H.

[3] See p. 58.

been forgotten by the Babylonians whose code is characterised by the frequent application of the death penalty." (*The Laws of Moses and Hammurabi*, p. 50, S. A. Cooke.)

Replacing the word Semitic by Adamite this opinion agrees with my own that the original rules given to Adam were perverted in Babylonia by Cain under the Devil's influence.

Cannibalism, like idolatry, is usually supposed to have been invented by savage and primitive tribes, but this opinion seems to be discounted by the fact that it was connected from the first with ritual and ceremonies.[1] The reason why it is not legislated against in the Laws of Moses is obviously because such a crime was unthinkable among the Hebrews,[2] while naturally it was not legislated against in the Code of Hammurabi because it was practised by the priests. The " ceremonial meals of Nintu of Kis,"[3] to which mysterious references are made in the Code of Hammurabi, were in all probability cannibalistic feasts such as those which horrified the first discoverers of Mexico ; for the ancient civilisation of that country is attributed to the Children of the Sun and there are strong reasons to connect it with that of Babylonia.[4]

One link between the ancient Babylonian civilisation and the Children of the Sun is that in the colonies founded by them the knowledge of an " All-father " seems always to have existed side by side with the worship of grotesque deities, just as in Babylonia the knowledge of God existed in the beginning of history, although creatures of man's imagination were worshipped.

[1] " Most kinds of cannibalism are hedged round with ceremonial regulations," and " We are justified in referring all forms of endo-cannibalism to a ritual origin." (*Ency. Brit.*, Ed. II, Cannibalism.)

" It is true that there are indications that human flesh had once been consumed in honour of the spirits of the earth, as Prof. Maspero has lately shown must have also been the case in pre-historic Egypt." (*Hibbert Lectures*, p. 83.)

[2] According to some commentators, the prophet Micah (iii, 3) accuses the Israelites of cannibalism, and it may well be that, influenced at one time by their Canaanite neighbours, they adopted that practice along with other idolatrous customs. Moloch and Chiun, the gods worshipped by the Canaanites (Amos v, 26), probably represented the Devil and Cain.

[3] Nintu was Ishtar (' the Lady of the gods "). (*Deluge Stories*, p. 63. L. King.)

[4] See Appendix D.

Even among the Bushmen of Australia, to which land Sir Arthur Keith tells us Asiatics journeyed by sea many thousands of years ago,[1] an " All-father " to whom a truly Divine nature is ascribed is secretly honoured, while public worship is given to a god represented by the praying-mantis insect which, very suggestively, is called alternately Cagn or Ikkagan;[2] and, as already mentioned, when the tradition of the Sun-god reached the Pacific Islands his name had reverted to " Kane."

> " Other evidence . . . suggests that the Children of the Sun originally ruled over Tahiti. . . . It is said that formerly some of the chiefs claimed descent from the great god Kane, evidently a sun-god."
>
> " The Iku-pau were direct descendants of ' Kane ' the god, or Kumuhenua the first man, . . . Kane being a sun-god, the Iku-pau would therefore be of the Sun, and thus ancient Hawaiian society falls into line with that of the archaic civilisation in general." (*The Children of the Sun*, pp. 167-311, W. J. Perry, 1923.)

Explorers admit the probability that the archaic civilisations of America, Australia, India and Oceania came originally from either Babylonia, Egypt or Northern Palestine; but how that civilisation first came into existence, and the origin of its mingled culture and barbarism must, I believe, remain a mystery unless the theory is accepted that Cain was the human original of the Sun-god whose followers wandered into every clime, carrying with them the culture of the ancient Babylonians and the leaven of malice and wickedness as well.

---

[1] Lecture at the Royal College of Surgeons, January 24th, 1925.
[2] *Ency. Brit.*, Ed. II, Mythology. See Appendix D.

V

MORE ABOUT KING CAIN

FURTHER information about Sargon of Akkad will naturally interest anyone who accepts my theory that he was Cain. The close alliance between Sargon and the Devil, attested to by the Babylonian inscriptions, agrees with what Josephus has to say about Cain's after life :

> " However he did not accept of his punishment in order to amendment but to increase his wickedness ; for he only aimed to procure everything that was for his own bodily pleasure, though it obliged him to be injurious to his neighbours." . . . " The posterity of Cain became exceedingly wicked, everyone successively dying one after another, more wicked than the former." (*Antiquities of the Jews*, II, 3.)

What the inscriptions say about Sargon indicates that he could, by putting his marvellous knowledge into practice, " procure everything that was for his own bodily pleasure," and also that he constantly made war against his neighbours, the other branch of Adam's race.[1]

Babylonia is known to have been exceedingly productive in ancient times on account of the elaborate system of irrigation of which traces have been discovered ; and, as we have seen, it was to Merodach (Cain ?) that that system was traced. Professor Leonard King, writing about the luxuries of Sargon's period, says :

> " Thus we read of the despatch of gold to Akkad, or of herds of oxen, or of flocks of sheep, lambs and goats. In return we find that Akkad sent grain and dates southward, and probably garments and woven stuffs ;

[1] See above pp. 25-144.

the importance of the first two exports is indicated by the frequent occurrence of the expressions ' grain of Akkad ' and ' dates of Akkad '[1] in the commercial texts." (*Sumer and Akkad*, p. 237.)

Alluding to Sargon as Shar-gani-sharri, the same writer describes his maritime activities ; and since he ascribes the Babylonian civilisation to the Sumerians and not to Cain he naturally pictures Sargon profiting by the long experience of Sumerian seamen in his naval expeditions, and prefers to think that Sargon organised rather than inaugurated the system of communication by water known to have been carried on in his reign : he writes :

> " From the earliest periods we know that the rivers and canals of Babylonia were navigated, and the Persian Gulf was a natural outlet for the trade of the Sumerian cities in the South. In organising a naval expedition for the conquest of the coast and the islands, Shar-gani-sharri would have had native ships and sailors at his disposal, whose knowledge of the Gulf had been acquired in the course of their regular trading. . . . In the internal administration of his empire Shar-gani-sharri appears to have inaugurated, or at any rate to have organised, a regular system of communication between the principal cities and the capital." (*Sumer and Akkad*, p. 235.)

But putting aside the possibility that Sargon was Cain and was endowed with superhuman knowledge it seems incredible that the great Sargon, as described upon the tablets, should have been prompted in any way by the inferior race (" the black-heads ") over whom he ruled.

The *Cambridge History* says of Sargon that :

> " In his third year he invaded the west. . . . He claims to have subdued the whole of the western lands and to have crossed the western sea, that is the Mediterranean, by which he may mean an occupation of Cyprus. From the ' land of the sea ' he caused booty to be brought over."

[1] We have noticed that the Sun-god is called "lord of the date." p. 83.

The same writer says that although Assyriologists have been reluctant to believe in these accounts of Sargon's voyages (and since they regard him as an ordinary human being, this is not surprising) his conclusion is that :

" It seems impossible to explain away the voyage of Sargon across some part of the Mediterranean, and naturally Cyprus was his first objective. Moreover, a stele of Sargon's son, Naram-Sin, has been found at Diarbekr." (Vol. 1, p. 405.)

Another writer says of Sargon :

" He is also stated to have made successful expeditions to Syria and Elam, and that with the conquered peoples of those countries he peopled Akkad, and built there a magnificent palace and temple, and that on one occasion he was absent three years when he advanced to the Mediterranean, and, like Sesotris, Hercules, etc., left there memorials of his deeds, returning home with immense spoils." (*Chaldea*, p. 205, Ragozin.)

VI

WAS CAIN IN CRETE?

ALTHOUGH Professor King hesitated to believe all that the Babylonian inscriptions say about Sargon's voyages, he shows that other authorities have arrived at startling conclusions upon the subject :

> " Not content with leaving him [Sargon] in Cyprus, Professor Winckler has dreamed of still further maritime expeditions on his part to Rhodes, Crete and even to the mainland of Greece itself." (*Sumer and Akkad*, p. 345.)

Further, he admits that :

> " There are, however, certain features of Ægean culture which may be traced to a Babylonian source. . . . The houses in Fara, for instance, are supplied with a very elaborate system of drainage, and drains and culverts have been found . . . at Nippur, at Surghul, and at most early Sumerian sites where excavations have been carried out. These have been compared with the system of drainage and sanitation at Knossos." (*Sumer and Akkad*, p. 345.)

He also says that " probably the clay tablet and stilus reached Crete from Babylonia."[1]

Professor Sayce tells us that a hæmatite cylinder found in Cyprus is inscribed with the name of Sargon's son, Naram-Sin, and that, " the divine title is prefixed to the royal name."[2] In the *Cambridge History* we read that Babylonian cylinders have been found in tombs in Cyprus which are supposed to belong to the third millennium before Christ,[3] and that :

---

[1] *Sumer and Akkad*, p. 345.
[2] *Hibbert Lectures*, 1887, p. 278.
[3] *Cambridge History*, Vol. I, p. 143.

" the omens of Sargon say definitely that he crossed
the sea of the West." (Vol. I, p. 405.)

These statements show that Professor Winckler's " dream "
of Sargon's presence in Crete was not unjustified ; and the name
of Khyan or Kian[1] (Cain) upon an alabaster lid of a coffer
discovered at Knossos in Crete[2] is yet another indication that
Sargon (i.e. Cain) was once there.

What would Professor King have said to the still more surprising claim now put forward that Sargon's empire included
part of Britain ?

> " A contemporary reference to the . . . tin mines
> in Britain appears probably to exist in the historical
> road-tablet of the great ' Akkad ' emperor Sargon I,
> . . . recording the mileage and geography of the
> roads throughout his vast empire of world-conquest.
> The existing document is a certified copy in cunei-
> form script of the original record of Sargon I. It
> was found at the Assyrian capital of Assur, and
> was made by an official scribe in the 8th century B.C.
> The tablet details the lengths of the roads within
> Sargon's empire from his capital at Agade on the
> Euphrates, and records that ' the produce of the
> mines in talents, and the produce of the fields to
> Sargon has been brought.' And it states that his
> empire of ' the countries from the rising to the setting
> of the sun, which Sargon the . . . king conquered
> with his hand,' included amongst many other lands
> . . . the Tin-land country which lies beyond the
> Upper Sea (or Mediterranean)."[3] (*The Phœnician
> Origin of Britons*, L. A. Waddell, LL.D., C.B., C.I.E.,
> etc., 1925, p. 413.)

and on page 160 Professor Waddell writes :

> " And it now seems that the ' Tin-land beyond the
> Upper Sea ' or (Mediterranean) of the Amorites [*sic*]
> subject to Sargon . . . was the Cassiterides of Corn-

[1] See Appendix D. The same name was found upon a granite lion in Babylonia (British Museum). *Cambridge History*, Vol. I, p. 175.
[2] *Greek Art and National Life*, Kaines Smith, p. 43.
[3] Text published in *Keilschrifttexte aus Assur verschiedenen Inhalts*, 1920,
No. 92.

wall." While another recent writer brings forward evidence for the Cretan origin of " megalithic England."[1]

Granted that Sargon of Akkad was Cain, and that he lived more than 700 years and possessed superhuman powers of body and mind, we find a clue to the problem of the pre-historic civilisation of Crete, Cyprus and Greece, and possibly of Britain, since the monuments seem to show that Sargon travelled to all these places. What more likely explanation can we find for the persistent traditions of " the first Sea-King " of whom a recent writer says :

> " Both Herodotus and Thusydides have preserved
> the record of the belief that a Cretan king called
> Minos was the first Sea-King known to history."
> (*The Life of the Ancient East*, J. Baikie, 1923.)[2]

The name Minos resembles that of Menes which is now thought to have represented not one, but a whole dynasty of Egyptian kings who according to Dr. Elliot Smith and other authorities came from Asia,[3] and according to Dr. Hall were " akin to the Cretans."[4]

One writer says :

> " In the word ' Minos ' we have, not the name of
> a single man, but the title of a race of Kings." (*Life
> of the Ancient East*, p. 369, Rev. J. Baikie.)

Now almost the same thing is said about Mena the traditional first king of Egypt,

> " It would seem that ' Mena ' in reality represents
> the early conquering monarchs of his dynasty."
> (*Ancient History of the Near East*, Dr. Hall, p. 105.)

and these remarks unintentionally support my theory that both the names Minos and Mena represented the race of Adam, and distinguished that race from the pre-Adamites of Crete and

---

[1] *Downland Man.* H. J. Massingham.

[2] If Sargon was this first Sea-King and was represented as Merodach, the trident with which that god is portrayed may be the original of Neptune's emblem. See picture, p. 91.

[3] *The Ancient Egyptians*, p. 118, 141.

[4] *Ancient History of the Near East*, p. 87.

Egypt. The early Cretans are called Minoans, and Dr. Hall connects them with the first Egyptian rulers (the Men or Menti of the monuments[1]) who according to Dr. Elliot Smith came from Asia.[2] This points to the fact that the names Minoan in Crete, Minyan in Armenia (in which country the Ark is believed to have rested[3]), Men in Babylonia[4] and Mena, Men, or Menti in Egypt distinguished Adam's race from the negroid inhabitants of those countries.

However this may be, the following description of Minos of Crete and his servitor Dædalus is interesting, because it fits Cain and his sons' sons' son Tubal-Cain. Mr. Baikie writes:

> " The Minos with whom we are most familiar in Greek story is not the righteous lawgiver and friend of God, but a very mundane ruler indeed. He is the great tyrant of the Ægean, sending out his fleets, and exacting his dreadful tribute from all lands ; he is the patron of Dædalus, the father of all artificers and inventors, who made for his master the gruesome brazen man Talos, and who built the dancing ground of Ariadne in Knossos, and reared the famous labyrinth." (*Life of the Ancient East*, p. 369.)

Is it too fanciful to suggest that Dædalus was Tubal-Cain, " an instructor of every artificer in brass and iron " (Gen. iv, 22), and that his brother Jubal, who " was the father of such as handle the harp and organ " inspired the Terpsichorean art of Ariadne ?

Accounts of Cretan art correspond so closely with what is said about Babylonian art that it seems necessary to trace both to the same origin, especially as they existed in the same millennium. The following remarks should be compared with those on page 30 :

> " One of the most amazing revelations of the excavations at Knossos was that of the artistic quality of the race of the Sea-Kings . . ."

[1] *Ancient History of the Near East*, p. 87.
[2] Ancient Egyptians.
[3] See Appendix B.
[4] *The Tel Armarna Tablets*, Conder, p. 174. " The land of the Men is said to have been near Assyria."

Speaking of one example, and quoting Sir Arthur Evans, the same writer says:

" As a work of art it is superb in its realism and vigour. ' No figure of a bull,' says Evans, ' at once so powerful and so true, was produced by later classical art '." (*Life of the Ancient East*, J. Baikie, p. 382.)

In Cretan art as in that of Babylonia the outstanding feature is the wilful degradation of true artistic ability and taste. The following remarks might equally well be applied to such Babylonian seals as those on pp. 62 and 67. Mr. Baikie says:

" There goes the revelation, not only in the great frescoes, but even more in such work as the seal impressions . . . of a strange, weird, unpleasant twist in the Minoan nature. There was something perverted and unhealthy in the fancy which designed some of the nightmare figures on these seals, whether their significance was religious or merely fantastic." (P. 39.)

That the hall-mark, as it were, of Cretan art was the serpent, helps to connect that degraded art with Cain. H. J. Massingham says:

" Indeed we have in Crete, where the imagination sprouted and sported as it did in no other country of the ancient world, an infinite variety of dragon-forms. . . . It is in Crete, too, that the serpent-cult of Egypt, represented by the sacred Uræus, reached its apogee. . . . And the serpent was certainly one of the prototypes of the dragon, as was the griffin, stone images of which stood in the throne-room of Minos. And when the mainland of Greece was fertilised with the cultural traditions of the Late Minoan period, we have the dragon-sceptre of the Mycenaean kings, another indication of the inter-relationship of kingship and dragonhood." (*Fee, Fi, Fo, Fum*, p. 102, 1926.)

Another link between Crete and the Babylonia of Sargon's

K

time is the dress of the women depicted upon the seals. It seems that, whether in Babylonia or Crete, the ladies of Sargon's court, dressed much like those of Queen Victoria's. The Babylonian drawing reproduced illustrates this.   (See p. 121.)

And of the Cretan women one writer says :

> " The attire of the ladies was staggeringly modern.
> . . . Evening dress, extremely low-cut, puffed
> sleeves, skirts elaborately flounced from hem to
> waist, hair wonderfully frizzed and curled. . ."
> (*The Life of the Ancient East*, p. 381, Rev. J. Baikie.)

Unintentional evidence of a connection between the religions of Crete and Babylonia comes from two independent writers ; one of whom writes :

> " The mystic philosophy known as the Gnossis was
> in all probability the philosophy taught in prehistoric
> times at Gnossis in Crete." (*Archaic England*, p. 76,
> H. Bailey.)

The other writer says that certain features of Gnosticism can be traced back to Babylonia, and that the seven evil spirits credited by the Gnostics with the creation of the world are the same as the seven evil spirits of the Babylonian inscriptions who (as we have seen)[1] are said to have created the first woman.

If Professor Waddell is right in identifying the " Sumerian Father-god " Zagg with the Cretan god Zeus[2] he, too, offers a link between the Babylonian and Cretan religions. We have already seen that Sargon was perhaps sometimes called Zagg-isi,[3] so probably both Zagg and Zeus were mythological representatives of him.

Surely the mere possibility that King Minos was Cain (and the most incredulous will, I think, admit that posibility) increases the interest of Crete and its buildings. We are told "that the Palace of Knossos was the home of an advanced knowledge of practically applied science, with its complex and skilful system of surface drainage, and well contrived light-areas in

---

[1] See p. 59.
[2] *Phœnician Origin of Britons, etc.*, p. 342.
[3] See p. 38 and Appendix D, p. 1.

the midst of its blocks of buildings," that it "presents a bewildering complex of walls, chambers, courts, and corridors, well meriting the name of Labyrinth," that " in its labyrinthine rooms and corridors are paintings of mighty bulls, and of eager and excited crowds of men and women," that Minos, its king, "was a mighty law-giver" and " that the throne-room has been discovered " with the "royal throne set against the wall and surrounded by the benches of his counsellors." (*Greek Art and National Life*, pp. 15-25.)

Another writer says :

> " It took the European world more than three thousand years to regain the sanitary knowledge which was lost when the Minoan Empire collapsed." (*Life of the Ancient East*, p. 392, Baikie.)

Mr. Kaines Smith comments upon one curious feature of Knossos :

> " Now the almost complete absence of fortifications at Knossos argues a feeling of security from attack which could only have arisen from a very high state of civilisation, and in addition, from a knowledge of superiority to most enemies. . . . Nor was attack feared from the sea, only a few watch-towers protect the palace. From this fact the only possible deduction is that Crete held dominion overseas." (*Greek Art, etc.*, p. 29.)

My suggestion is that Crete was, on the contrary, an oversea colony of Babylonia and that the absence of fortifications was due to the fact that Adam's descendants, through Seth, never interfered with Cain's career. I picture the Sethites in the territory eventually destroyed by the Deluge, living as peacefully as Cain's raids[1] upon them and their own ever-increasing wickedness allowed.

The fact that the ruins of several palaces have been excavated in Crete, built on the same lines, although at intervals of centuries, supports the theory that Cain, who lived for centuries, was their architect ; and the following statement helps my

[1] *Sumer and Akkad*, p. 249, L. King. See pp. 132-144.
[1] Excavated by the French School of Athens.

argument by showing that there once lived in Crete a priest-king of gigantic size who is suspected of sacrificing human beings and, perhaps, of cannibalism.

Sir Arthur Evans is reported as saying :

" The discoveries which had been made by the French were of extraordinary interest. They found that the rooms in which the ruler lived—he was certainly a priest-king—were on one storey and that windows looked out upon an open corridor. Facing the central court was a raised stone platform, or loggia, approached by steps and with part of an altar on the top of it. The priest-king evidently went up from his rooms on the inside and showed himself to the people in the central court, and no doubt he performed certain rites or addressed the people. In a little room the French investigators had found a pot which could be dated about 2100 B.C. and an immense bronze sword longer than any ancient sword known in Europe. The sword was a beautiful fabric, gold plated on the hilt and ending in a faceted crystal knob, which had a certain amount of amethystine colours, and it evidently belonged to the King-priest. Fragments of bone, which would probably prove to be human, were also found. There had been discovered also a bronze axe, the back of which was formed in the shape of a leopard and was covered with spiral ornamentation. This was a ceremonial axe that had belonged to a cult which came over, no doubt, from Asia Minor, and it was apparently the badge of the King's dignity as priest, as the sword was the badge of his civil power. These formed the first remains that had been found of one of the early prehistoric kings." (*Times* newspaper, November 11th, 1925.)

Seeing that Sargon of Akkad may be traced to Crete and that the civilisation of that island is dated back to Sargon's period (according to the monuments)[1] and to Cain's (according to the Bible dates) it may be confidently claimed that no more

[1] *Ency. Brit.*, Ed. XI, Crete. " The successive ' Minoan ' strata, which go well back into the fourth millennium B.C."

reasonable explanation is to be found for its pre-historic glories than that Cain with his superhuman knowledge once ruled there. If those fragments of bone are really human, they, as well as the mighty sword and the ceremonial axe, may be sinister links with the " first murderer." As the priest-king of Enlil what ghastly rites may he not have performed upon that platform in sight of his cringing courtiers? Were the Babylonian priests serious or ironical when they wrote of Sargon that " he poured out his glory over the world ? "[1]

[1] *Sumer and Akkad*, p. 234.

VII

THE SAD END OF SARGON

A LATE Jewish tradition describes Cain in his last days as a
fugitive and a terrible spectacle, having grown a long horn
upon his forehead.[1] He is said to have been mistaken for a
wild beast while lurking in a thicket and to have been shot
by his blind descendant Lamech. Whether there is any truth
in that story or not, it certainly appears from the garbled
fragments of the priests' writings that the " Babylonian
Charlemagne " fell on evil days. According to Professor King,
one of Sargon's inscriptions says :

> " Because of the evil which he had committed
> the great Marduk was angry and he destroyed his
> people by famine. From the rising of the sun unto
> the setting of the sun they opposed him and gave
> him no rest. . . . It may seem strange that such an
> ending should follow the account of a brilliant and
> victorious reign. But it is perhaps permissible to see
> in the evil deeds ascribed to Sargon a reference to
> his policy of deportation which may have raised him
> bitter enemies among the priesthood and the more
> conservative elements in the population of the
> country." (*Sumer and Akkad*, p. 240.)

The theory that Sargon was in the habit of deporting his subjects encourages the assumption that Cain's civilisation and
customs were early spread abroad.[2]

In the *Cambridge History* we read :

> " The glorious reign of Sargon closed with the
> entire empire in revolt. The Babylonian Chronicle

[1] Perhaps the story of the horn arose from the fact that Sargon wore a
horned helmet resembling that seen in the drawing given above of Sargon's
son. Professor King says : " He wears a helmet adorned with the horns of
a bull, and he carries a battle-axe and a bow and arrow." (See illustration
facing.)

[2] *Sumer and Akkad*, L. King, p. 242.

NARAM-SIN, WITH HORNED HELMET [See p. 142.

Reproduced from King's " A History of Sumer and Akkad," by permission of the Publishers, Messrs. Chatto and Windus.

[Photo : W. F. Mansell.

[Face p. 142.

pragmatically attributes his disaster to the violation of the holy city Babylon. An Omen text preserves the same tradition: ' Sargon whose troops bound him in a trench and suppressed their master in a coalition.' The misfortune which overtook him at the end of his career is again referred to a birth omen, ' If an ewe give birth to a lion with head of a lamb, lamentation of Sargon whose universal dominion (passed away) '." (P. 408.)

Cain's successor seems to have been called Naram-Sin and to have been as great a warrior as Sargon; he claims the proud title of " King of the four quarters (of the world) "[1] and is said to have conquered nine armies.[2] Professor King says:

> " There can be little doubt that Shar-gani-sharri was succeeded on the throne of Akkad by Naram-Sin, whom we may regard with considerable confidence as his son as well as successor . . ." (*Sumer and Akkad*, p. 241.)

Considering the unreliable character of the priestly writings it is impossible to know whether these kings did everything which the inscriptions suggest; but if they were Cain and his son they might well have done wonders, for presumably they were superhuman.

Sargon's dynasty had evidently come to an end about the year 2400 B.C. when a king called Samu-abi (Shem is my father) is known to have conquered Babylonia,[3] and to have founded the dynasty of which Hammurabi the reputed contemporary of Abraham was the last king. This dynasty is naturally considered to have been of the race of Shem; and although Assyriologists have inserted several conjectural dynasties based upon " Sumerian " names between Samu-abi and Sargon, my conviction is that Cain's descendants reigned in Babylonia until they were finally driven out by Shem or his sons. God was to " dwell in the tents of Shem " (Gen. ix, 27) and unquestionably Shem's descendants were the preservers of the Divine oracles from the time of Noah; it is therefore very

[1] *Sumer and Akkad*, L. King, p. 242.
[2] *Times History*, Vol. I, p. 363.
[3] Ussher's date for the Deluge is about 50 years later, but considering that such early dates are only approximate this disparity is negligible.

probable that Shem's tribe attacked Babylonia (the stronghold of idolatry). And if the later Babylonian priests disguised the fact that servants of the One God had once conquered and reigned in their land, and preferred to suggest that Cain's rule ended in a revolution of his own subjects, it is only what we should expect from them. That Noah's sons brought about the downfall of Cain's empire is suggested by the monuments which show that the people against whom Sargon and his son fought in Western Asia were of the same race as themselves and not black people as Sargon's subjects seem to have been.

Describing the stele of Sharru-gi (another form of the name Sargon), Professor King says :

> " The king's enemies are Semites so that even in his time we have the picture of different clans or tribes contending among themselves for the possession of the countries they had overrun." (*Sumer and Akkad,* p. 249.)

That no black enemies appear in the war pictures of the period justifies the conclusion that when " the Children of the Sun-god " wandered eastwards in search, as it is thought, of gold, pearls, and turquoise, they met with no resistance from any black races they may have encountered, and peacefully founded civilisations as Cain had first done in Babylonia. All except one of the great ancient civilisations have long passed away, but the remaining one has so many characteristics in common with Sargon's empire that some allusion to it is irresistible, and that the Yellow race owes its origin to " a very early blend " of Cain's race with a black race is a proposition quite in accordance with Ethnological doctrines.[1]

[1] *Ency. Brit.,* Ed. XI, Ethnology.

VIII

WAS CAIN THE FOUNDER OF CHINA?

THE suggestion that Cain or his near descendants founded the mysterious Chinese empire may, at first sight, be regarded as fantastic, but Chinese traditions and other considerations offer ground for such a theory.

Just as Sargon of Akkad is said to have ruled over the black-heads, so in Chinese tradition the first ruler is said to have " transformed the black-haired people " and to have made them " brightly intelligent."[1]   Just as Cain, if my deductions are correct, brought the knowledge of One God into Babylonia, but substituted for His worship the worship of his own parents, so we find that in China both the knowledge of One God and the worship of ancestors existed as far back as history can reach.

In the *Encyclopædia Britannica* we read that :

> " The earliest traces of religious thought and practice in China point to a simple monotheism. There was a Divine Ruler of the universe, abiding on high, beyond the ken of man. . . . Gradually to this monotheistic conception was added a worship of the sun, moon and constellations, of the five planets, and of such noticeable individual stars as (e.g.) Canopus, which is now looked upon as the home of the God of Longevity. . . . Side by side with such sacrificial rites was the worship of ancestors, stretching so far back that its origin is not discernible in such historical documents as we possess. . . . This ancestor cult is not a memorial service in simple honour of the dead ; but has always been, and still is, worship in the strict sense of the term." (Ed. XI, Vol. 6, p. 174.)

[1] *Sacred Books of the East*, Max Muller, p. 32.

A more recent writer says :

" The origin of the Chinese is shrouded in obscurity Some suppose that the ancestors of the Chinese first lived in the territory south of the Caspian Sea and migrated eastward somewhere about the 23rd century B.C. Others assert that their original home was in Babylonia on the great Euphrates plain, and that they derived many of the elements of their civilisation from the ancient Chaldeans. . . . it seems certain that they travelled from the western part of Asia and made a settlement first of all in what is now known as the modern province of Shensi in the Valley of the Yellow River. After their migration they soon took up agricultural pursuits and ceased to be a pastoral people. Among the most primitive characters of the Chinese written language, we find hieroglyphs which point to the conclusion that they not only kept sheep and cattle but also engaged in tilling the soil. In many ways the construction of a Chinese house bears a strong resemblance to that of a tent, and this gives the idea that the Chinese were originally a nomadic or wandering people. The Chinese were not the first inhabitants of the country in which they settled. Upon migrating to the valley of the Yellow River they found aboriginal tribes already in possession and obtained the territory from them by conquest. These native tribes were pressed more and more south and west but were never exterminated."
(*Sketch of Chinese History*, F. Hawkes Pott, p. 23.)

The same writer says that the earliest rulers " brought all the culture of China," that to them was due its Golden Age, and (which is suggestive in connection with Cain) one of those earliest rulers was known as the " Divine Agriculturist."[1]

The late Professor Terrein de Lacouperie claimed a great similarity between the Babylonian and Chinese beliefs and institutions, in their astronomy and medicine, and drew attention to the fact that recent excavations in Babylon show that :

" the canals and artificial waterways of China suggest

[1] *Golden Bough*, Vol. 2, p. 12.

a striking likeness to the canals with which the whole of Babylonia must have been intersected, and which must have been as characteristic a feature of that country as similar works in China at the present day." (*China*, Professor K. Douglas.)

One grim sign that the Chinese civilisation was derived from Cain is that, according to old historians, cannibalism existed among the ancient Chinese.[1]   It could hardly have been taken there by the Hamites for they seem to have gone into Africa, nor is there any reason to suspect the family of Japhet of spreading evil, or for that matter of building up great civilisations ; the descendants of Shem, judging by all we hear of them in the Bible, were incapable of such barbarism, and we may therefore conclude that cannibalism was taken into China from Babylonia by some of Cain's race, or even perhaps by Cain himself.

It must be granted that these are solid grounds for thinking that the Chinese civilisation originated in Mesopotamia, and there is further evidence of this.   Several writers believe that the Chinese language has some affinity with the primitive language of Babylonia, and Professor Sayce quotes Professor de Lacouperie as saying that the ancestors of the Chinese were in contact with the inventors of the cuneiform system of writing, while he himself traces the oblique eyes peculiar to the Chinese back to Babylonia, saying :

> " The earliest Babylonian monuments give two types of man, one with oblique eyes and negrito-like face, the other heavily bearded." (*Archæology of the Inscriptions*, Sayce.)

Just as Cain's arrival in Babylonia seems the simplest explanation of the sudden advent in that country of civilisation and culture, so his influence would account, as nothing else could do, for the Chinese art, philosophy and science which are known to have existed at the beginning of their history.

That a people who have never changed or advanced and are in some ways so barbarous and so diabolically cruel should have

[1] *Ency. Brit.*, p. 184, Ed. XI. Cannibalism.

possessed the knowledge of good and evil from the first is a problem only to be explained by this theory about Cain, which receives more unintentional support from Professor Douglas, who says :

> " There is nothing improbable in the supposed movement of the Chinese tribes from Mesopotamia to the banks of the Yellow river." (China.)

Trifling as the following indications may seem, they help to support my theory. We have seen that the title of " Divine Agriculturist " was known in ancient Chinese history. Is it perhaps in memory of Cain, the first " tiller of the ground," that the Chinese Emperor has from time immemorial opened the ploughing for the year in the " sacred field," sometimes called the " field of God ? "

Sir James Frazer says :

> " The emperor attended by the highest dignitaries of the state, guides with his own hand the ox-drawn plough down several furrows and scatters the seed in a sacred field, a field of God." (Golden Bough, Vol. II, p. 12, Ed. 2.)

Again, was it to Cain's 730 years' lease of life that the Emperor Ho-ang-ti referred[1] when lamenting the comparative shortness of life in his own time ; and is that long lifetime commemorated by the Chinese of to-day (unconscious though they may be of the fact) in their Hall of Imperial Longevity, their god of longevity, etc. ?

The name China itself, and the names Chang, Chien, Chuen, Kan, Kieng, etc., all resembling the name Cain, as well as Kha-khan, the title of the chief Mongol, are noteworthy ; as is also Sin or Sing resembling the " sin " of Naram-sin.

Again, for straws show which way the wind blows, the Chinese Imperial title, Ruler of the Yellow, the coveted order of the Yellow Jacket, the Yellow tiles of the Imperial palaces and the temples, the Yellow Imperial colour and the Yellow River are all curiously suggestive considering that, for some unknown reason, yellow is Cain's traditional colour. Shakes-

[1] See p. 33.

BABYLONIAN GOD

See p. 43.

BABYLONIAN
DRAWING,
SMALL HEAD
(Compare with
Frontispiece.)

See p. 43.

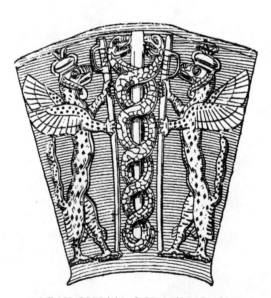

BABYLONIAN LIBATION CUP   [See p. 149.

The above illustrations are reproduced from King's " A History of Sumer and Akkad," by permission of the Publishers, Messrs. Chatto and Windus.

[Face p. 149.

peare wrote : " a little beard, a Cain-coloured beard " ;[1] and in ancient tapestries Cain's beard is always yellow.

And what of China's Dragon, " the symbol of the Sage and of the King," the Deity alternately praised and blamed, blessed and cursed, the emblem of the Emperor in his Dragon robes upon his Dragon throne before his Dragon tablet ?   Surely in the Dragon of China we find another link with Babylonia and with Cain, for were not King Cain's subjects called the Children of Bel and was not Bel the Dragon ?   In Babylonia, upon the libation vases of the temples were depicted fabulous reptiles. In China (as one writer says) the Dragon is intimately associated with the element of water,[3] while in Babylonia Bel sometimes appeared as Akki the water-carrier or irrigator.

Professor Douglas writes :

> " The chains of hills which almost encircle Peking are called the protecting Dragon, which is believed to ensure the city's prosperity.   The mound built behind a tomb to keep off the north wind is called the Dragon."   (*China.*)

This digression upon the Chinese empire, which may be thought irrelevant, is warranted I feel, by my firm conviction that while, humanly speaking, Babylonia owed to Cain the Golden Cup which was to make the nations mad, China owes to him its emblem the Dragon—" the old serpent, called the Devil, and Satan, which deceiveth the whole world."   (Rev. xii, 9.)   (See illustration facing.)

[1] Brewer's *Dictionary of Phrase and Fable.*
[1] Professor Elliot Smith writes : " At a very early date both India and China were diversely influenced by Babylonia, the great breeding place of dragons " (p. 102) and (p. 95, footnote).   " There can be no doubt that the Chinese dragon is the descendant of the early Babylonian monster and that the inspiration to create it reached Shensi during the 3rd millennium B.C. (*The Evolution of the Dragon.*)

[3] See Appendix I.

IX

EVIDENCE SUMMED UP

THE evidence that Cain was Sargon may then be summed up as follows :

The fact that Sargon's achievements imply both a degree of wisdom and power unparalleled in history, and a long life, such as is traditionally ascribed to Cain.

The extraordinary ability combined with depravity of Sargon's government and activities, so consistent with all that is known of Cain.

The probability that the Babylonian city of Erech or Unuk was the city of Enoch built by Cain. (See p. 27.)

The fact that the city is often mentioned in inscriptions in connection with Sargon, and is called " the seat of the worship of Anu and Isthar " (the deified representatives of Adam and Eve) ; and that it was " in the court of Sargon " that the worship of those gods was first established.   (See p. 71).

That Sargon's date was about 3800 B.C., at which time Cain, according to the Bible dates, may have been alive.

That the second syllable of Sargon's name is the same as Cain, and the first syllable means a ruler or King.

That while St. John says that Cain was " of that wicked one," Sargon is called the " king-priest of Enlil " (the Devil) ;[1] is shown to have been adopted by Akki (the Devil) ;[2] and is made to call his father " Dati-Enlil " (the Devil).[3]

That his arrival is described in a legend as sudden and mysterious, as Cain's arrival in Babylonia must have been.

That Sargon, like Cain, ruled over a race different from himself.

[1] *Cambridge History*, Vol. I, p. 408.
[2] See p. 94.
[3] See p. 95.

That Sargon is called the " king of the city,"[1] whereas Cain, according to the Bible, built a city.

That Sargon is called " the Founder," the " constituted " or " pre-destined king," the " Deviser of constituted law and Deviser of prosperity " or the " very wise," all of which might well have described Cain.

That Sargon is represented in inscriptions as the gardener of Anu (Adam), as Beloved of Isthar (Eve) and only loved by her for a certain period, since he says : " When I was a gardener Isthar loved me," which may refer to the fact that after the murder of Abel, Eve renounced Cain.

That Sargon is called the son of Ea (Eve)[2] and, under the name of Merodach the Sun-god, is constantly called the first-born of Ea, is shown to be the brother of Tammuz (Abel) and (as Adar) to have killed Tammuz.

That while Sargon's subjects are called the black-heads, Merodach, whom I regard as the mythological representative of Cain, is said to have ruled over the Igigi or Nigil (ma), probably negroes.

It must be remembered, too, that the theory of Cain's presence in Babylonia offers the best explanation for the sudden arrival in that country of a marvellous civilisation and culture, and relieves us of the necessity of believing that it was gradually evolved by an inferior race ; that it seems to be the key to the Sumerian problem—to the problem of the origin of idolatry—to the problem of the ancient civilisations attributed to the Children of the Sun-god—and to be the best explanation of the Roman Custom which Sir James Frazer makes the keynote of " The Golden Bough." Finally, it explains, as nothing else can do, how the knowledge of God and of His laws was taken into Babylonia in the very earliest times and how that knowledge came to be suppressed or travestied almost beyond recognition.

---

[1] *Hibbert Lectures*, Sayce, p. 28.
[2] *Worship of the Dead*, Garnier, p. 399.

X

THE PICTURE PUZZLE MADE

PUTTING together all this evidence we can picture Cain—a superman—heir to supernatural knowledge, who (we infer) had spoken face to face with some Divine Messenger—going forth alone in agony of mind among an unknown and dreaded race. A Jewish history says:

> " Cain dwelt in the earth trembling according as God had appointed him after he slew Abel his brother."[1]

But it adds " and he began to build cities " and " he founded seven cities," which indicates that new courage came to him; and the Babylonian inscriptions show whence it came. According to them it was the Devil who adopted Sargon and in exchange for his worship and obedience gave him power and wealth.

Perhaps the scribe who wrote: " the evil spirit hath lain wait in the desert, unto the side of the man hath drawn nigh,"[2] hinted darkly at the temptation and fall of Cain, who must have become " of that wicked one " and must have drunk deep of the Golden Cup before he built sanctuaries to Adam and Eve in his city of Enoch, thus breaking the greatest of God's commandments. Can we not imagine Cain surrounded by his " sons of the palace " clothed like Merodach upon the monuments—riding over mountains in bronze chariots[3]—conquering and to conquer—floating in some stately barge from one of his seven cities to another while his pre-Adamite subjects toiled in the plains which he, by his irrigation works, had transformed

---

[1] *Biblical Antiquities of Philo*, p. 77. Trans. by M. R. James.
[2] *The Devils and Evil Spirits of Babylonia*, R. Thompson, Vol. II, p. 105.
[3] Sargon says: " In multitudes of bronze chariots I have rode over rugged lands . . . three times to the sea I advanced." (*Hibbert Lectures*, Sayce, p. 27.)

into the garden of the ancient world ; or exploring the seas with a fleet of many-oared galleys, landing on distant shores, discovering mines, founding settlements and building stupendous palaces and temples ?   Can we not picture him conducting hideous ceremonies upon a stone platform like that recently found in Crete, wielding a ceremonial axe (perhaps the very one discovered on that spot),[1] and offering human sacrifices to the Devil, or presiding at cannibal orgies of a ritualistic nature, such as were carried on up to the sixteenth century by the Children of the Sun-god in America ?

And his end ?   Was not Cain the foremost of all the " wandering stars for which the blackness of darkness hath been reserved for ever ? "[2]

Here ends my effort to show that in the grey dawn of history men possessed the knowledge of God ; that that knowledge, while preserved by the descendants of Seth, was taken by Cain into Babylonia and there corrupted, together with the story of the Garden of Eden ; that the mythological literature of that country is full of veiled references to that story and that, therefore, the theory that the first chapters of Genesis were founded upon Babylonian myths may be dimissed as groundless.

Constant attacks of all kinds are made in the Press upon the authenticity of those chapters : Sir Oliver Lodge has lately lamented the fact that the universal adoption of the theory of evolution is retarded by the lingering belief in the Divine inspiration of the Old Testament, which he claims is " literature and must be judged by literary standards only."[3]   Since, however, as I have tried to show, the Old Testament provides answers to problems which are otherwise unsolvable, it surely deserves to be regarded as more than literature even by scientists.

Under the title " The Problem of Unbelief," the following words appeared in the *Times* newspaper of March 19th, 1925 :

> " The intelligensia, in spite of its being daily more
> conscious of the failure of mere accumulation of know-

[1] See p. 140.
[2] Epistle of Jude v, 13.
[3] Evolution in Everything, *Daily Express*, July 23rd, 1925.

L

ledge to solve the riddle of the Universe and of human destiny, refused to turn to the Church because it had not been persuaded to think that the Church had any answer worth considering to offer."

The strong conviction that the answer to that riddle can only be found in the Old and New Testaments has inspired this little work.   Was not the Scottish poet of early Victorian days wiser than our modern evolutionists when he wrote :

" Within that awful volume lies
    The mystery of mysteries
Happiest they of human race,
To whom God has granted grace
    To read, to fear, to hope, to pray,
To lift the latch and force the way ;
    And better had they ne'er been born,
Who read to doubt, or read to scorn."

SCOTT.

APPENDIX A (p. 9.)

THE TESTIMONY OF SCIENCE

THE agreement of scientific discoveries with the sequence of events of the Creation of the World, described in the Bible as occurring during the seven periods (so-called days), is denied. We read : " that the records of the pre-historic ages in Genesis are at complete variance with modern science and archæological research is unquestionable." (*Encyclopædia Britannica*, Ed. II. Genesis.) Yet the agreement of the Bible statements with modern science was attested to by scientists in the last century, and as far as I can ascertain no later discoveries have discredited their judgment.

Dr. Kinns, Ph.D. (University of Jena), who published a list of the scientists who had approved his work, points out that the events of the Creation of the Bible narrative are fifteen in number, and the evolution of the world as admitted by those scientists can also be divided into fifteen stages. Since a mathematical calculation shows that the chance of accidentally reproducing the exact relative sequence of any fifteen units is about one to a million million, the most sceptical must allow the improbability, to say the least of it, of the exact reproduction of either of these sequences being accidental. . . Yet their agreement is proved by science. The following is Dr. Kinn's comparison of the events of the Creation as attested to by the Bible on the one side and on the other by modern science :

> *Primarily :* Science says that matter existed first in a highly attenuated gaseous condition, called æther, without any form, and non-luminous.
> *Moses says :* " And the earth was without form, and void, and darkness was upon the face of the deep."

155

I. Science : The condensation of this æther formed luminous nebulæ, which afterwards still further condensed into suns and worlds.

Moses : " And God said, Let there be light."

II. Science : In this condensation of nebulæ astronomical facts go to prove that other worlds were formed before the Solar System.

Moses : " God created the Heaven and the Earth."

III. Science : On the cooling of the earth some of the gases which surrounded it, combined mechanically and chemically to form air and water.

Moses : " And God said, Let there be a firmament."

IV. Science : On further cooling great convulsions took place, which heaved up the rocks and raised them above the universal sea, forming mountains, islands and continents.

Moses : " And God said, Let the dry land appear."

V. Science : The earliest forms of vegetable life were cryptograms, such as the algæ lichens, fungi, and ferns, on the land, these are propagated by spores and not by seeds. Dr. Hicks has found ferns in the lower silurian of Wales.

Moses : " And God said, Let the earth bring forth grass." Literal translation : Let the earth sprout forth sproutage, which might be rendered tender herbage.

VI. Science : Next succeeded the lowest class of phænogams, or flowering plants called gymnosperms, from having naked seeds, such as the conifers. Dana mentions coniferous wood found in the lower Devonian.

Moses : " The herb yielding seed."

VII. Science : These were followed by a higher class of Phenogams, or flowering plants, bearing a low order of fruit, found in the Middle Devonian and Carboniferous strata.

Moses : " And the fruit tree yielding fruit." The higher order of fruit trees appeared when " God planted a garden " later on.

VIII. Science : The earth until after the Carboniferous period was evidently surrounded with much vapour, and an equable climate prevailed all over its surface; afterwards these mists subsided, and then the direct rays of the sun caused the seasons.

Moses : " And God said, Let there be lights in the firmament of heaven, and let them be for signs and for seasons."

IX. Science : After the Carboniferous period many fresh species of marine animals appeared, and the seas swarmed with life.

Moses : " And God said, Let the waters bring forth abundantly."

X. Science : In the New Red Sandstone footprints of birds are found for the first time.

Moses : " And fowl that may fly above the earth."

XI. Science : In the after strata of the Lias, monster Saurians such as the Ichthyosaurus and Plesiosaurus are found.

Moses : " And God created great whales." Should have been translated " sea monsters."

XII. Science : Enormous beasts, such as the Megalosaurus, Iguanodon, and Dinotherium, preceded the advent of cattle.

Moses : " And God made the beast of the earth after his kind."

XIII. Science : Cattle, such as oxen and deer, appeared before man; some of them in the Post-Pliocene period.

Moses : " And cattle after their kind."

XIV. Science : According to Agassiz, the principal flowers, fruit trees, and cereals appeared only a short time previous to the human race.

Moses : " The Lord God planted a garden . . . and out of the ground made the Lord God to grow everything that is pleasant to the sight and good for food."

XV. Science : The highest and last created form of animal life was Man.

Moses : " And God created man in His own image."

Finally : Science : As far as our present knowledge goes, no fresh species of plants or animals were created after man.

Moses : " God ended His work which He had made."

In these ways, as Dr. Kinns points out, the book of nature supports the Bible. Sir John Herschel once wrote: " All human discoveries seem to be made only for the purpose of confirming more strongly the truths that come from on high and are contained in the sacred writings."

TOO HASTY CRITICISMS

In the *One Volume Bible Commentary* (Genesis) the writer says: " Assuming that the astronomers are right, or, indeed, on any reasonable proposition, the sun and moon were not created later than the earth." But does the Bible say they were? Is it not evident that verse 16 of the first chapter, in which the sun and moon are mentioned, refers back to the creation of the great light called Day described in the first verse? Could that light have been any other than the sun? That it was so, one translator of the Bible makes clearer by rendering verse 16 as " And God had made two luminaries," and by rendering the first verse: " By periods, God created that which produced the suns ; then that which produced the earth."[1] Thus rendered, these verses harmonise with the modern theory of the solar system. Dr. Kinns shows that where we read in Gen. i, 16, " God made two great lights," reference is made to the period when the dense vapours that first surrounded the earth disappeared, enabling the light and heat of the sun to reach it. He shows that the word " made " may equally well be rendered " appointed " as in the 104th Psalm, verse 19: " He appointed the Moon for seasons, and the Sun knoweth his going down."

Another writer, referring to the Creation and Fall of Man, the sentence on mankind, etc., says:

" The discoveries of the immensities of the universe, of the antiquity of man, and of the compilation of the Old Testament between 458 and 140 B.C. cut away the whole foundation of this theology."

But, I would ask this writer, where does the Bible upon which " this theology " is founded, deny the immensity of the

[1] Ferrer Fenton, *The Bible in Modern English.*

universe or limit the antiquity of the pre-Adamites in whose existence it leads us to believe. And what proof is there that the Bible Records were not handed down both in writing and orally in an unbroken line from Adam ?—I can find none.

APPENDIX B (p. 18)

" THERE is another wrong impression—that the ark rested upon the top of Mount Ararat. The Bible does not say so, but that it rested upon the *mountains* of Ararat. Now the ark could not have rested upon several mountains, but it might float on to a portion of this chain of mountains, and be left there some feet above the ground when the waters subsided. In Mr. George Smith's translation of the ' Deluge Tablet,' we find it stated that ' the mountain of Nizir *stopped* the ship ; and to pass over it, it was not able.' " (*Moses and Geology*, S. Kinns, p. 399.)

APPENDIX C to D (p. 25)

AN INTERESTING POSSIBILITY

ACCORDING to inscriptions and drawings Sargon was constantly at war with people of his own race ; we may conclude, therefore, that he came into collision with the other branch of Adam's family. He is said to have brought captives of war into Babylonia and in this way probably raised the standard of the population. Professor King writes : " The people of Elam which was situated east of Mesopotamia were, from an early period, in constant conflict with Babylonia." (*Books on Egypt and Chaldea*, Vol. IV, p. 157.)

The name " Elam " marks Cain's adversaries as a non-Cainite branch of Adam's family, for Elam was a son of Shem ; but it is, of course, an anachronism when applied to people of Sargon's time, if Sargon was Cain, and if, as seems practically certain, " Elam " was called after Shem's son, who lived long after Sargon's death. The loose way in which Biblical names are used has been remarked upon. (See p. 14.)

One wonders how the Deluge, which destroyed the Adamites affected Cain's nation in Babylonia. It is at least suggestive that in Dr. Moffat's new version of the Old Testament we find that when the Adamites came to " an untimely end [1]: when the floods undermined them, good men rejoiced to see their fate, and over them the guiltless jeered, shouting ' Our foes are now effaced, and what they leave the flames will burn.' " As it is difficult to imagine Noah and his family regarding the rest of Adam's race (the Sethites) as their foes, the question arises—can Cain and his followers be alluded to ? There is scope for investigation in the fact that the Hebrew word translated guiltless is Naqi or Naqah which resembles the word Akki or Akkad—Should it have been rendered " Akkadians " instead of " guiltless " ? It is easier to picture Sargon's descendants and their followers shouting " our foes are now effaced, and what they leave the flames will burn " than to believe that Noah and his family could be so inhuman.

According to the Bible dates, the Deluge took place about the year 2348 B.C. so Shem's descendants and those of Cain may have come into conflict, for a " Semitic " king called Samu-abi (Shem is my father[3]) overthew some Babylonian dynasty about that time.[3] And it seems possible that Shem's son Assur, who is said in the Bible to have gone forth from the Land of Nimrod and to have built Nineveh, was that Shemitic king. The reason why Nimrod was ruling in Babylonia at that time may be that he was the last representative of Cain's dynasty if, as Bishop Cumberland surmised,[4] his grandfather Ham took as his wife Naamah, Cain's woman descendant ; Nimrod may have succeeded to the Babylonian throne through her. According to Josephus and other Jewish traditions Nimrod was a bad man—what more natural, therefore, than that Shem's son

[1] Job xxii, 16-20.
[2] *Times History*, Vol. I, p. 363.
[3] *Times History*, Vol. I, p. 327.
[4] *Sanchoniathon's History*, p. 107, Cumberland. The writer says that according to Plutarch, the wife of Cronus (the mythological form of Ham), was " Nemaus," which he says would be just the Greek form of the Hebrew " Naamah," the only woman descendant of Cain mentioned in the Bible.

should have descended upon him, driven him out, and reigned in his stead? He may have escaped to Egypt, for there is reason to think that he was the human original of the Egyptian god Osiris[1]; and the name Nimrod appears in Egyptian inscriptions. If his grandfather and father went down into Egypt as the fact that that land was called after them both seems to prove, it would naturally have been his place of refuge. Considering all this it is not difficult to imagine how Cain's evil customs arrived in Egypt and, as some writers have suggested, passed on even into Mexico.

Just as the priests blurred their picture of the Sun-god Merodach (whom I identify with Cain) by giving him another name, varying his attributes and inventing, in later times, two other Sun-gods, so they have blurred their picture of Sargon by ascribing his achievements to other rulers bearing " Sumerian " names. As we have seen, for instance, " Enmerkar "[2] to whom they ascribe the building of Erech is obviously Sargon under another name if Professor Sayce is right in thinking that Cain built that city[3] and if I am right in believing that Cain was Sargon. In the same way a king called Lugal-Zaggisi is said to have " consolidated and ruled an empire extending from the Persian Gulf to the Mediterranean "[4]; and even Professor King who regarded Lugal-Zaggisi as a real and separate individual, says that although Sargon achieved all that, there are " difficulties in the way of crediting Lugal-Zaggisi with a like achievement."[5] We have seen that Professor King admits that Sargon's history is the one point in early Babylonian history certainly established.[6]

Colonel Garnier, who considers that Lugal-Zaggisi was only another name for Sargon, points out that both Lugal-Zaggisi and Sargon are said to be the king of Erech and the high-priest of En-lil, that they both say that En-lil bestowed upon them their lands and subjects, that they conquered " from the Upper

---

[1] *Worship of the Dead*, p. 36. " Nimrod also appears to have been the human original of the Egyptian ' Osiris '."
[1] See Appendix D, p. iv.
[2] See p. 34.
[3] See p. 27.
[4] *Sumer and Akkad*, pp. 197-198.
[5] See p. 35.
[6] *Sumer and Akkad*, p. 198.

Sea to the Lower Sea," and that they are " the mighty man, son of the god Ea, prince of the Moon-god, begotten of Tammuz and Isthar."[1]   " Hence," as Colonel Garnier says, " Lugal-Zaggisi is the Great Lord (or king) Sargina."[2]

The fact that the names of Lugal-kigub-ninidudu and Lugal-kisalsi are found upon a door-socket attributed to Sargon suggests that they, too, were other names applied to Sargon and Colonel Garnier identifies the first name with Sargon.[3]   All this helps to show how the Babylonian priests tried to make things difficult.[4]

Another instance of the priests' inconsistencies commented on in the *Cambridge History*, Vol. I, p. 403 :

> " Of Sargon, founder of the Semitic dynasty at Agade, many romantic stories were current. Two chronological tablets state : ' At Agade Sharru-kin-lubani, a gardener and cup-bearer of Ur-Ilbaba, having been made king, ruled 55 years.' "

In a footnote the following comment is made : " But Ur-Ilbaba was the third king of the fourth dynasty of Kish and is assigned a reign of eighty years (according to another tablet, six years) and as five other kings of Kish and the reign of Lugal-Zaggisi intervene with a total of eighty-six years, Sargon cannot have been the king's cup-bearer. . . . It was a posthumous cult of Ur-Ilbaba at Kish in which the young Sargon officiated."   I submit that the name Ur-Ilbaba was only one of the names invented by the priests who disguised the true history of Ancient Babylonia, that, as Colonel Garnier, was the first to suggest, Lugal-Zaggisi was another name for Sargon; that the " other five kings " were fictitious; and that we see in the discrepancy described above an example of how the priests' inscriptions puzzle and mislead us unless we realise that they were meant to mystify posterity.

In connection with my theory that Cain's superhuman knowledge was spread over the world by his descendants it is at least curious that the pioneers of iron-working in Borneo are

[1] *Worship of the Dead*, p. 399.
[2] See p. 93 and *Worship of the Dead*, p. 399.
[3] *Sumer and Akkad*, p. 199.
[4] See p. 59.

called " the Kayan " and that their ancestors are said to have been " a gang of criminals,"[1] although it was apparently they who taught the aborigines of Borneo the art of working in metal. One writer says :

> " In any account of the arts and crafts of the Kayans the working of iron claims the first place by reason of its high importance to them and of the skill and knowledge displayed by them in the operations by which they produce their fine swords. The origin of their knowledge of iron and of the processes of smelting and forging remains hidden in mystery (!) ; but there can be little doubt that the Kayan were familiar with these processes before they entered Borneo." (*Children of the Sun*, W. J. Perry, p. 122.)

There are indications that some of Noah's family travelled from Babylonia to Egypt and thence across Africa to America. The *Encyclopædia Britannica* (Ed. XI) says " that on account of those indications the first Spanish explorers of Mexico arrived at the curiously definite result that the Mexicans were descended from Naphtuhim, son of Mizraim and grandson of Noah who left Egypt for Mexico shortly after the confusion of tongues." Naturally, since the Bible History is ignored by modern scholars, the writer continues " modern archæologists approach the question from a different standpoint," although he seems to support the theories held by the Spaniards by adding that " the original peopling of America might . . . well date from the time when there was continuous land between it and Asia."

One indication that the Babylonian civilisation went into Egypt is that the oldest pyramid (that of Sakkarah) is, like the Babylonian towers, built in terraces ;[2] and that it penetrated into Mexico is indicated by the facts that the " Mexican belief in the stages of heaven and hell was apparently learnt from the Babylonian-Greek astronomical theory,"[3] and that : " not long ago Dr. Thomas Gann announced that Dr. H. J. Spinden, of Harvard, had discovered definite proofs of the exact

---

[1] *Children of the Sun*, p. 110.
[2] *Hist. of Egypt*, Birch, p. 25.
[3] *Ency. Brit.*, Ed. XI, Mexico, p. 330.

year from which the ancient Maya builders of Central America dated their time-count, namely 3373 B.C.,"[1] a discovery proving that the Mayan civilisation existed at a time when, according to the Bible and monumental evidence combined, Cain (i.e. Sargon) may have been reigning in Babylonia is, to say the least, significant.

The architecture and decorations of the ancient Maya buildings are strangely reminiscent of Chinese art.

And one writer says :

> " The jade beads dug up amid Aztec remains probably had their origin in China, the nearest point where such jade is found. The bronze figure exhumed in the old tomb at Oaxaca is undoubtedly Chinese." (*Mexico as I saw it*, Mrs. Alec Tweedie, p. 161.)

These facts suggest that there was intercourse between China and Mexico in ancient times, and that Babylonia was the go-between seems likely, for a few drawings found there are unmistakably Chinese in style,[2] while pottery lately discovered in China resembles Babylonian work. We read in *Discovery, A Monthly Journal of Knowledge*, December, 1926 :

> " The discovery of such pottery in China created a sensation among European archæologists. The manner of its manufacture, its general appearance, . . . all recalled the pottery found on neolithic and early Bronze Age in Eastern Europe and Western Asia . . . at Susa, at Ur, . . . Interesting speculations were at once suggested. Was China after all connected with the Near East in its very early days ? . . . Was there a common origin for the neolithic inhabitants of both extremities of the Asiatic continent ? "

In connection with Professor Waddell's information quoted on page 134, it is interesting that he links up the Babylonian goddess with the British " Queen of the May," whom he also connects with the "Maia of the Greeks, Mahi and Maya of the Vedas and Indian epics "; and he suggests that the

---

[1] *Discovery. A Monthly Journal of Knowledge*, June, 1925.
[2] See portrait of Marduk with dragon, Mesopotamia, by L. Delaporte, p. 140 (Berlin Museum).

ancient May Day festivities included human sacrifices and cannibalism. He writes :

> "Thus we have the vestiges of this sacrificial so-called Beltane rite surviving in Britain on May Day with the ceremonial sacrifice of a boy victim by lot." (p. 271.)

and mentions : "the prevalence of cannibalism amongst savage tribes in Britain."

It seems probably, therefore, that English merry-makers have unconsciously commemorated grim ceremonies once held by Babylonian immigrants in these islands in honour of the Devil ; and that the May-pole was cousin-german to the sacred tree of the murderer priest-king of Nemi. Happily, Britons need not own descent from the importers of Babylonian names and customs; for archæological research is showing more and more distinctly that the builders of Avebury and Stonehenge came here (and apparently passed away) before the arrival of the Brythons, Cymbri, Celts and other tribes whom we may safely claim as our ancestors.

APPENDIX E (p. 58)

PROFESSOR SAYCE writes :

> "That human sacrifices, however, were known as far back as the Accadian era, is shown by a bilingual text (K 5139) which enjoins the *abgal*, or 'chief prophet,' to declare that the father must give the life of his child for the sin of his own soul, the child's head for his head, the child's neck for his neck, the child's breast for his breast." (*Hibbert Lectures*, p. 78, 1887.)

APPENDIX F (p. 101)

THAT the art of irrigation was taken into Egypt by Noah's family seems a likely proposition in view of the facts that Egypt was called after Ham and Mizraim, that the Egyptian god

Amon was probably the mythological representative of Ham,[1] and that the latest anthropological discoveries show that a ruling race went down into Egypt from Syria or Armenia at the very beginning of history.[2] If, as seems probable, Ham was the first Egyptian ruler we may reasonably assume that human sacrifice and cannibalism (both of which were practised in Egypt) were instituted by him, for from all we gather about him from the Bible and ancient records, he " went in the way of Cain."

APPENDIX G (p. 54)

The hymn to Enlil reminds one of the answer given by the controlling spirit of a modern medium. When asked, " Do you know of any such spirit as a person we call the Devil? " the reply was, " We certainly do, and yet this same Devil is our God, our Father." (From *Spiritualism*, by the Rev. H. R. Anderson, M.A.)

APPENDIX FA (p. 109)

SIR JAMES FRAZER writes: " Apuleius, when he was initiated into the mysteries, says that Isis, the Egyptian Isthar, revealed herself to him in the following words: ' I am nature, the parent of things, mistress of the elements, the beginning of ages, sovereign of the gods, Queen of the manes, the first of heavenly beings. My divinity uniform in itself is honoured under different names, various rites, the Phrygians call me Persimuntca " mother goddess " the Cecropians " Minerva " the people of Cyprus " Paphian Venus," the arrow armed Cretans, " Diana Dictyana," the goddess who divines the secret of the gods." (Golden Bough). Here we find Diana connected with Isthar and surely her title (as above) refers to Eve and the fruit of the Tree of Knowledge.

[1] *History of Sanchoniathon*, Bishop Cumberland, p. 99.
[2] *Ancient Egyptians*, Professor Elliot Smith.

APPENDIX H (p. 127)

PHILOLOGY is often regarded as a broken reed to lean upon, and the following suggestion may be thought fantastic, but seeing that Cain was probably the instigator of "cannibalism" is it not possible that that word was derived from him? The writer quoted below gives his opinion that the probable derivation of the word is cahna bal, " the priest of Bal," cahna being the emphatic form of cahn " a priest."

Very suggestively Josephus calls priestly garments Cahanaeae. (Antiquites of the Jews, Book III, c. 7.)

" The word cannibal is said by some to be derived from Carib, the name of the people of the Caribbean Islands. But the derivation is very forced and unnatural. Shakespeare used ' cannibal ' as a well-recognised term in his time for eaters of human flesh, and as the West Indies had only been discovered ninety to a hundred years before and the name of ' Carib ' was not known until much later, it could hardly have been corrupted into ' cannibal,' nor is there the slightest evidence that such a forced and unlikely corruption ever took place."[1]

This writer offers no new theory regarding the name " cannibal," perhaps if he, too, had regarded Cain as the first high priest of Bel, and the inventor of the ghastly custom of eating human flesh, he might also have suggested that the word was derived from Cain.

APPENDIX I (p. 149)

THE Dragon of China is believed to have power to give or to withhold rain. " On one occasion there was a long and severe drought which the Dragon refused to mitigate in spite of prayers and curses lavished upon him. As, notwithstanding numerous processions, the Dragon persisted in not sending rain, the indignant Emperor launched against him a thundering edict, and condemned him to perpetual exile on the borders of the river Ili, in the province of Torgot. The sentence was

[1] Hislop, *Two Babylons*, p. 232.

about to be executed and the criminal was proceeding with touching resignation to cross the deserts of Tartary, and undergo his punishment on the frontiers of Turkestan, when the supreme courts of Pekin, touched with compassion, went in a body to throw themselves at the feet of the Emperor and ask pardon for the poor Devil." (*Chinese Empire*, by M. Huc.)

CPSIA information can be obtained
at www.ICGtesting.com
Printed in the USA
BVHW091448080422
633567BV00006B/471